The Drucker Foundation
Self-Assessment Tool

PROCESS GUIDE

Revised Edition

Gary J. Stern

Introduction by Peter F. Drucker

Foreword by Frances Hesselbein

The Drucker Foundation
New York • www.pfdf.org

Jossey-Bass Publishers
San Francisco • www.josseybass.com

Jossey-Bass books and products are available through most bookstores. To contact Jossey-Bass directly, call (888) 378-2537, fax to (800) 605-2665, or visit our website at www.josseybass.com.

Substantial discounts on bulk quantities of Jossey-Bass books are available to corporations, professional associations, and other organizations. For details and discount information, contact the special sales department at Jossey-Bass.

ISBN: 0-7879-4436-X

Library of Congress Catalog Card Number 98-67792

This book is printed on paper containing a minimum of 10 percent postconsumer waste and manufactured in the United States of America.

Interior design by Gene Crofts

PB Printing   10 9 8 7 6 5 4   SECOND EDITION

Contents

PART ONE

The Drucker Foundation Self-Assessment Process

PART TWO

Step-by-Step Guidelines for Self-Assessment

Resources for Self-Assessment

Exhibits

Foreword: An Adventure in Organizational Self-Discovery

Self-assessment is a process of organizational self-discovery. It is a discussion about the future and how your organization will shape it, an intellectual and emotional adventure—for minds and hearts are involved. The *Self-Assessment Tool* is designed to guide and focus this journey into the future with Peter Drucker's Five Most Important Questions: *What is our mission? Who is our customer? What does the customer value? What are our results?* and *What is our plan?* To answer these questions, you will look outside the organization to opportunities and to what your customers value. And you will look inside to the organization's mission and to what you must do to achieve results.

The *Self-Assessment Tool* is flexible. As one customer describes it, "This is a living, breathing process of examination, improvement, and reexamination." The *Tool* is used by organizations in all three sectors, and portions of it are woven into a range of planning exercises. Here are four examples that demonstrate the *Tool*'s range:

• A task force within a national public health organization had been wrestling for months over the proper focus and design of a proposed network of research centers. The chairman reports, "Once we stepped back and affirmed the research centers' mission, defined our primary and supporting customers, and identified what they value, we had a new understanding and were quickly able to come to a decision all could support."

• Newly elected members join a suburban county's library board every two years. The board's semi-annual orientation and planning retreat begins with Peter Drucker's discussion and worksheets on mission. Said one member, "I have served on many boards, and I find it very healthy that in my first meeting there was sufficient time spent on the core reason this institution exists."

• A small community development agency used the *Tool* to conduct an organizationwide self-assessment in the face of rapidly changing community demographics. The executive director reflects on the resulting plan. "It was a lot of work, but it was satisfying work. The beauty of this structure is that it doesn't stop at the 'preferred future.' The methodology made the plan real and not just another brainstorming exercise."

• The *Tool* provided the format for field projects in an M.B.A. course titled "Organizational Management and Leadership." The students' "clients" included nonprofit organizations, businesses, a government agency, and two universities. A student writes, "This has been the most important motivating factor in helping me determine what I want to pursue once I graduate." The professor comments, "The projects helped organizations develop action plans that would make them more effective in the community or the business world."

Please define *your* purpose for using the *Tool* and adapt the self-assessment process to the needs and culture of your organization. *Make it your own.*

The Revised Edition

This new edition of *The Drucker Foundation Self-Assessment Tool* reflects significant feedback from our customers. We have made many changes based on their suggestions. One result is a streamlined Participant Workbook that provides greater focus for the reader as he or she explores Peter Drucker's introductions to the five questions and responds to accompanying worksheets. Our customers cautioned us that "it is too easy to go on our assumptions," and so the process now asks more in terms of going *outside* the organization. We strongly encourage engaging in direct research with your customers and conducting an "environmental scan" to discover facts and trends in the operating environment that are likely to affect the organization in its future work.

We heard a clear call for in-depth guidance in conducting the self-assessment process and for more information on implementing plans. This expanded Process Guide includes detailed instruction for each of three phases in the self-assessment process, reports and a completed plan, sample agendas for group discussions or a retreat, sample customer research formats, a process to develop a mission statement, guidance on facilitation, examples of adaptations of the process, and additional resources. As part of the Participant Workbook, Peter Drucker provides a new afterword titled "Beyond Good Intentions: Effective Implementation of the Plan."

We are deeply grateful to all those who commented on their experience with the *Tool* and for the opportunity to use the ideas of those with firsthand knowledge of what is valued: our customers.

A Journey into the Future

Remarkable opportunities exist for those who would lead their enterprises and this country into a new kind of community—a cohesive community of healthy children, strong families, good education, decent housing, and work that dignifies. These leaders will dare to see life and community whole. Rather than fret about a "shrinking piece of the old pie," nonprofit organizations with vision and new mind-sets will forge relationships crossing the private, public, and social sectors to build partnerships and community. *They will change lives.*

Peter Drucker's Five Most Important Questions go to the very heart of an organization—why it exists and how it will make a difference. They are the *essential* questions, and by asking them you will focus on excellence in performance and on what you must do to achieve it. The questions are not easy. We members of the Drucker Foundation board and staff ask them of ourselves periodically, and I know that when *you* ask these questions, all who participate in seeking answers will have an exuberant and valuable discussion.

The self-assessment process is an adventure in organizational self-discovery, a means for assessing how to *be:* how to develop quality, character, mind-set, values, and courage. On behalf of the Drucker Foundation, we offer this guide to your journey into the future and our encouragement to begin.

August 1998

Frances Hesselbein
President and CEO
The Peter F. Drucker Foundation
for Nonprofit Management

Acknowledgments

We are deeply grateful, first and foremost, to the hundreds of nonprofit executives, facilitators, and other customers who shared their experience and comments on the first edition of the *Self-Assessment Tool* and thereby helped us improve it. Our thanks again go to Constance Rossum for her original work on the self-assessment process and to the many individuals who contributed to the *Tool*'s initial development.

Our appreciation also goes to Steven Gray for customer research; to Steven Mayer for numerous insights; to Elana Centor for environmental scan research; to Barbara Raye for counsel on recommended reading and results; to Marilyn Marles for her retreat agenda; to Debbe Kennedy for her revised edition prototype; to Alan Shrader, our editorial partner at Jossey-Bass; to Rob Johnston for his skillful guidance of this project; and to Carol Dombeck, Juanita Lauritsen, Windy Block, Lynn Steenblock, John Roiger, and the entire board and staff of the Southwest Minnesota Private Industry Council for their wonderful work field-testing the revised *Tool*.

Many facilitators, consultants, leadership volunteers, and nonprofit executives contributed their time and ideas to this revised Process Guide. Our thanks to Terry Anderson, Emil Angelica, Dick Aft, Sara Barnes, Joseph Bergen, Jack Bradt, H. Yvonne Cheek, Libby Dietrich, Diane Espaldon, Joel Feldman, Alan Fischlowitz, Beth Fischlowitz, Pat Grazzini, Holly Hartstone, Mary Ann Johnson, Demetrios Karabetsos, Beverly Klegman, Sandra Larson, Carol Lukas, Jill

Markowitz, Gwendolyn Mister, Melba Moore, Louanne Peterman, Patricia Peterson, Suzanna G. Pollak, Vincent Pulskamp, Bob Soter, Marjorie Shapiro, Anne Smith, Steve Smith, and Ann Waterhouse.

Our final thanks go to the foundation's honorary chairman, Peter F. Drucker, for his decades of dedication to the effective organization, for his contributions to management literature, and for his support and contributions to the social sector.

GE Fund

Development of the revised *Drucker Foundation Self-Assessment Tool* was made possible in part by financial support from the GE Fund.

About Gary J. Stern

Gary J. Stern is president of Gary J. Stern & Associates, Inc., an international consulting firm specializing in organizational effectiveness with nonprofit groups. He is the author of *Marketing Workbook for Nonprofit Organizations, Volume I: Develop the Marketing Plan,* which was adapted as the official marketing workbook of United Way of America, and *Marketing Workbook Volume II: Mobilize People for Marketing Success.* Both are in circulation around the world.

Former senior consultant with the Amherst H. Wilder Foundation, Stern is a noted speaker and trainer. He has been a speaker at the Stanford University Graduate School of Business and at the Drucker Foundation Leadership and Management Conference, and his clients include the American Lung Association, the National Council of Jewish Women, United Way of Canada-Centraide Canada, YMCA-USA, and Fundacion Compromiso of Argentina. Stern is based in Minneapolis, Minnesota.

PART ONE

The Drucker Foundation Self-Assessment Process

Introduction

Social sector institutions are America's resounding success story of the last fifty years. They are central to the quality of life, central to citizenship, and indeed carry the values of American society and the American tradition. The pressure for effective community service will only grow as society continues through a period of sharp transformation. Out of a need for personal involvement, the number of Americans who volunteer will increase as well. The social sector organization is fast becoming the new center of social action, of active commitment, and of meaningful contribution.

An accomplished fact in today's environment, and a very healthy one, is the requirement that social sector organizations be accountable. *Changed lives* is the nonprofit organization's "bottom line." Each mission must be thought through in terms of results, and the organization must document the difference that is being made in society and in the lives of individuals. People are no longer simply interested to know, Is it a good cause? Instead, they want to see both commitment *and* competence—a demonstration of achievement as a responsible and effective organization.

The Five Most Important Questions

The self-assessment process is a method for assessing what you are doing, why you are doing it, and what you *must* do to improve an organization's performance. It asks the five essential questions: *What is our mission? Who is our customer? What does the customer value? What are our results?* and *What is our plan?* Self-assessment leads to action and lacks meaning without it. To meet growing needs and succeed in a turbulent and exacting environment, social sector organizations must focus on mission, demonstrate accountability, and achieve results.

You cannot arrive at the right definition of results without significant input from your *customers*—and please do not get into a debate over that term. In business, a customer is someone you must satisfy. If you don't, you have no results. And pretty soon you have no business. In a nonprofit organization, whether you call the customer a student, patient, member, participant, volunteer, donor, or anything else, the focus must be on what these individuals and groups value—on satisfying their needs, wants, and aspirations.

The danger is in acting on what *you* believe satisfies the customer. You will inevitably make wrong assumptions. Leadership should not even try to guess at the answers; it should always go to customers in a systematic quest for those answers. And so, in the self-assessment process, you will have a three-way conversation with your board, staff, and customers and include each of these perspectives in your discussions and decisions.

Planning Is Not an Event

When you follow the self-assessment process through to its completion, you will have formulated a plan. Planning is frequently misunderstood as making future decisions, but decisions exist only in the present. You must have overarching goals that add up to a vision for the future, but the immediate question that faces the organization is not what to do tomorrow. The question is, What must we do *today* to achieve results? Planning is not an event. It is the continuous process of strengthening what works and abandoning what does not, of making risk-taking decisions with the greatest knowledge of their potential effect, and of setting objectives, appraising performance and results through systematic feedback, and making ongoing adjustments as conditions change.

The First Action Requirement of Leadership

Your organization's commitment to self-assessment is a commitment to leadership development. You have vital judgments ahead: whether to change the mission, what opportunities match your competence and commitment, how you will build community and change lives. Self-assessment—this constant resharpening, constant refocusing—is the first action requirement of leadership.

In my fifty years of work with social sector organizations, I have known many outstanding leaders. One is a man I met quite by chance, a rabbi, who taught me by example that *you are responsible for allocating your life."* This is as true for organizations as it is for individuals. It is the underlying challenge of the self-assessment process. The question must continually be asked, Why does the organization exist? What, in the end, do we want to be remembered for? When you find answers, above all, I urge you to act on them.

August 1998

Peter F. Drucker
Claremont, California

Definition of Terms

Mission — Why you do what you do; the organization's reason for being, its purpose. Says what, in the end, you want to be remembered for.

Vision — A picture of the organization's desired future.

Customers — Those who must be satisfied in order for the organization to achieve results. The *primary customer* is the person whose life is changed through the organization's work. *Supporting customers* are volunteers, members, partners, funders, referral sources, employees, and others who must be satisfied.

Customer Value — That which satisfies customers' *needs* (physical and psychological well-being), *wants* (where, when, and how service is provided), and *aspirations* (desired long-term results).

Results — The organization's bottom line. Defined in *changed lives*—people's behavior, circumstances, health, hopes, competence, or capacity. Results are always *outside* the organization.

Goals — A set of three to five aims that set the organization's fundamental, long-range direction.

Objectives — Specific and measurable levels of achievement.

Action Steps — Detailed plans and activities directed toward meeting an organization's objectives.

Budget — The commitment of resources necessary to implement plans—the financial expression of a particular plan of work.

Appraisal Process for monitoring progress in meeting objectives and achieving results; point at which the plans for meeting objectives may be modified, based on experience or changed conditions.

There are four additional terms in the self-assessment process that may not be familiar:

Depth Interviews One-on-one interviews used to highlight the insights of a select group of individuals inside the organization. Interview findings provide a touchstone for group discussions and decision making.

Environmental Scan A process for discovering and documenting facts and trends in the operating environment that are likely to affect the organization in its future work. Environmental scan findings are used to orient self-assessment participants.

Internal Data Summarized information regarding the history, present status, and performance of the organization. Includes a current mission statement. Internal data are used to orient self-assessment participants.

Leadership Team The chairman of the board and the chief executive officer of a nonprofit organization. These leaders of the governance and management of the organization work together to make self-assessment possible.

Governance and Management in Self-Assessment

The Drucker Foundation Self-Assessment Tool is built upon a bedrock principle of nonprofit organizations: the clear and sharp differentiation of governance and management. The volunteer board of directors, trustees, or governors is responsible for the governance and policy of the organization. Management—whether professional staff employed by the organization or volunteers serving in operational roles—is accountable for the objectives and performance. Operating within these broad guidelines allows nonprofit organizations to achieve their highest performance. With the board chairman and the chief executive setting the standard for a productive partnership, organizations can, in Peter Drucker's words, succeed in "making people's strengths effective and their weaknesses irrelevant." The organization can focus on changing lives and building community. Following is a broad outline of the responsibilities of governance and the accountabilities of management that apply to the self-assessment process.

Responsibilities of the Governing Board	Accountabilities of Management
Leadership	*Leadership*
The board chairman and the chief executive form the self-assessment Leadership Team. The chairman recommends self-assessment to the board and later presents the mission, vision, and goals to the board for approval.	The board chairman and the chief executive make up the self-assessment Leadership Team. The chief executive coordinates self-assessment, presents objectives and action steps to the board for information, and the supporting budget for approval.
Strategic Planning	*Operational (Tactical) Planning*
The board sets the organization's direction through a clear mission, goals that describe its vision of the desired future, and oversight of the allocation of resources.	Management develops the objectives, action steps, and supporting budget for how the organization will achieve its goals and further its mission.
Appraisal and Oversight	*Performance*
The board reviews the annual and interim management reports. As legal stewards of the organization, the board carries specific fiduciary responsibilities and ensures the organization's compliance with laws and standards of practice.	Management is accountable for the organizational performance. It keeps the board informed in a timely manner about progress against projections and presents an annual management report.

The Self-Assessment Process

Outline

Phase One: Preparing for Self-Assessment

Design Option A: Two Group Discussions

1. Gain commitment from the board and management
2. Determine participants and process design
3. Form the Assessment Team
4. Select a facilitator and a writer
5. Announce the process, invite participation, and confirm key dates
6. Conduct an environmental scan and gather internal data

Design Option B: One Group Retreat

1. Gain commitment from the board and management
2. Determine participants and process design
3. Form the Assessment Team
4. Select a facilitator and a writer
5. Announce the process, invite participation, and confirm key dates
6. Conduct an environmental scan, conduct customer research and depth interviews, and gather internal data

Phase Two: Conducting the Self-Assessment Process

Design Option A: Two Group Discussions

1. Orient participants; distribute internal data, the Participant Workbook, and summary report on environmental trends and implications
2. Hold group discussion on the first three Drucker questions
3. Conduct customer research and depth interviews
4. Distribute customer research and depth interview reports and hold group discussion on the fourth and fifth Drucker questions
5. Prepare and distribute final report

Design Option B: One Group Retreat

1. Orient participants; distribute internal data, the Participant Workbook, and summary reports on environmental trends and implications, customer research, and depth interviews
2. Hold retreat
3. Prepare and distribute final report

Phase Three: Completing the Plan

1. Revise the mission (if needed); confirm goals and results
2. Develop objectives, action steps, and budget [management]
3. Prepare the plan for presentation to the board
4. Present the mission, goals, and supporting budget for board approval [Management presents objectives to board for information]
5. Distribute the plan, confirm responsibilities and dates for initial appraisal

Note: It is helpful to have reviewed the Participant Workbook in its entirety before continuing in the Process Guide.

The *Self-Assessment Tool* was originally developed to meet the need in the social sector for "a management resource . . . a method to help us think through what we are doing, why we are doing it, and what we *must* do." The moment one considers seriously the Five Most Important Questions—*What is our mission? Who is our customer? What does the customer value? What are our results? What is our plan?*—the experience of the Drucker "method" begins. It is much more than answering questions. The Drucker Self-Assessment Process converts knowledge into effective action. This means engaging the board, the staff, and your customers in a challenging process of organizational self-discovery. And as anyone who has been involved in a process of self-assessment or planning knows, the quality of the process becomes every bit as important as the discoveries themselves.

Before embarking on self-assessment, leaders must know why the organization is undertaking it, who should be involved, and how the process can be designed and managed to ensure that it is effective and rewarding. Customer research conducted for this revised edition called for the in-depth information and guidance necessary to structure a thorough self-assessment process and make it a success. Comprehensive organizational self-assessment—its phases, steps, and details—is therefore the centerpiece of this Guide.

Comprehensive organizational self-assessment takes place in three phases over a number of months (see process outline). Many, sometimes all, members of the organization participate at various points and in differing roles.

Phase One: Preparing for Self-Assessment

This first phase is devoted to organizing the process, gathering necessary internal and external information, and launching self-assessment. The board endorses the concept; the board chairman and chief executive design the process; an Assessment Team is formed to lead it—most often with the assistance of a facilitator and a writer. Management is responsible for moving the process forward.

There are two major design options for comprehensive organizational self-assessment.

Design Option A: Two group discussions

This option calls for successive sessions in which the Drucker questions are discussed and answered. Direct customer research and depth interviews occur in Phase Two between the first and second group discussion.

This option puts all self-assessment research into Phase One and calls for a single all-day session on the Drucker questions in Phase Two. Option A tends to be a lengthier process and provides greater opportunities for involvement. Option B can compress self-assessment into a shorter time period and places greater responsibility with the Assessment Team.

Phase Two: Conducting the Self-Assessment Process

This phase is centered around asking and answering Peter Drucker's Five Most Important Questions. Participant Workbooks and informational reports are distributed, followed by broad participation of board and staff members in facilitated group discussions or a retreat. There may also be opportunities for the board and the staff to take part in customer research and depth interviews in either Phase One or Phase Two.

Phase Three: Completing the Plan

This phase leads to board approval of the organization's vision, mission, goals, and supporting budget, as well as to management's development and implementation of objectives and action steps. The Assessment Team or a special task force prepares a revised mission statement (if needed); the Assessment Team confirms goals and results, and the chief executive oversees the involvement of staff or operating volunteers in developing draft objectives, action steps, and budgets. The board chairman presents the plan for board approval.

A Flexible Process

This Process Guide offers both structure and flexibility, shows how to be inclusive yet efficient, and reflects principles of effective group process, sound management, and good governance. The book has two major sections. The first is the step-by-step guide to a comprehensive organizational self-assessment. The Resources section that follows provides additional guidance. The Process Guide is the companion to the Self-Assessment Participant Workbook that is referenced throughout.

The *Self-Assessment Tool* can be adapted to any organizational setting, and portions are used to meet a variety of needs (see Resource 1 for four examples of adaptations). Customers of the *Tool* report variations that range from using a single worksheet to focus a discussion in a meeting, to using the process to help organize a new nonprofit organization, to making self-assessment the means for program evaluation and planning throughout an entire county. Please adapt the *Tool* to your particular needs, and accept the encouragement to *make it your own*.

PART TWO

Step-by-Step Guidelines for Self-Assessment

Preparing for Self-Assessment

Phase One establishes the foundation on which you can build a successful self-assessment process. The board chairman and chief executive determine who will be involved and what participants will do. They sketch the steps from initial meetings to board approval of a plan, gain commitment to the process, and inform every member of the organization that self-assessment is being undertaken and why. Phase One concludes by gathering essential external and internal information that you can use to orient self-assessment participants to the journey ahead. The six steps in Phase One are:

1. Gain commitment from the board and management.
2. Determine participants and process design.
3. Form the Assessment Team.
4. Select a facilitator and a writer.
5. Announce the process, invite participation, and confirm key dates.
6. Conduct an environmental scan and gather internal data. (With Design Option B: One Group Retreat, customer research and depth interviews are also conducted at this point.)

Overview of Phase One

Step 1: Gain commitment from the board and management

The board chairman and chief executive define the purpose of undertaking self-assessment and lead the effort. The *Self-Assessment Tool* is designed to engage board members throughout the process and to properly delegate decision-making authority between governance and management. Because self-assessment addresses fundamental aspects of governance—mission, overarching goals, the right allocation of resources, and production of meaningful results—the formal decision to initiate the process is made by the board of directors. The chief executive ensures the commitment of management and is responsible for the process.

Step 2: Determine participants and process design

The board chairman and chief executive outline who the participants in the self-assessment process will be, decide an overall time frame, and develop a detailed process design.

Step 3: Form the Assessment Team

In most organizations, the board chairman and chief executive are joined by additional members of an Assessment Team to oversee and carry out the self-assessment process. In Step 3, this group is formed and holds its initial meeting to develop understanding and move the process forward.

Step 4: Select a facilitator and a writer

The self-assessment process engages participants in group discussions to expand their vision and tighten their focus. Major decisions are debated—and the decisions *should* be controversial. In this step, selecting a skilled and objective facilitator from either inside or outside the organization will help ensure that discussions are constructive; the facilitator can also conduct depth interviews and potentially consult in other ways. One or more writers are also needed to handle the five to seven self-assessment writing projects.

Step 5: Announce the process, invite participation, and confirm key dates

In Step 5, everyone who is part of the organization is informed that self-assessment is being undertaken. In addition, direct invitations are given to those being asked to fill out Participant Workbooks and participate in group discussions, a retreat, or depth interviews. To build understanding of the self-assessment process and ownership for the resulting plan, initial announcements and explanations should be the first of regular progress reports and briefings throughout the process.

Step 6: Conduct an environmental scan and gather internal data

Through an environmental scan, key facts and trends in the environment can be discovered that are likely to affect the organization in its future work. Internal data are gathered and summarized to orient participants to the mission, history, and present status of the organization. This information is used to educate self-assessment participants on the organization and the context within which the mission is to be carried out. In Step 6, the environmental scan is designed and conducted, internal data are gathered, and a summary report of findings is developed. (If following Design Option B: One Group Retreat, customer research and depth interviews are also conducted at this point.)

Detailed Steps

STEP 1   Gain commitment from the board and management

Board members and staff approach self-assessment with varying degrees of understanding, enthusiasm, or concern. The topic may prove controversial. Some people have had poor prior experiences with self-assessment or planning and consider it a waste of time. Others may speak against it because they are concerned about change and would prefer not to make any, whereas others want a chance to present revolutionary ideas. For many individuals, the concept of systematic self-assessment is simply new, and they need to understand more about the process, its purpose, and its implications before they can endorse it.

Meetings at which self-assessment is proposed should allow sufficient time for explanation and discussion. It may be helpful to distribute copies of the Foreword and the Introduction to this Process Guide, as well as the process outline shown in The Self-Assessment Process, in advance. The board chairman and chief executive should prepare by looking ahead to Step 2, which is to determine participants and process design; they should outline their thoughts regarding the purpose for undertaking self-assessment, the ways board and staff will be involved, the key elements of the process design, and a general time frame.

Board commitment to self-assessment fulfills a fundamental responsibility of governance. As trustees of a social sector organization, the board is ultimately responsible for the mission, the overarching goals, the effective allocation of resources, and the achievement of meaningful results. The *Self-Assessment Tool* is designed to engage board members throughout the process, to properly delegate decision-making authority between governance and management, and to make appropriate use of board members' time.

It is the role of the chairman to propose self-assessment to the board. Once the board is committed, it is the responsibility of the chief executive to ensure that the process is effectively carried out and to engage the full participation of management and staff. Ideally, *all* those asked to participate will wholeheartedly support self-assessment, but even if they do not, their commitment means they understand what is asked of them and agree to do it.

STEP 2   Determine participants and process design

The decision to initiate self-assessment is made by the board of directors. The board chairman and chief executive design and lead the effort. *They determine the following:*

- The organization's purpose in undertaking self-assessment
- Self-assessment participants and process design, including a time frame
- A budget for the self-assessment process, if needed

It is helpful to consult others in the organization in these preparations and, in some cases, to select a facilitator if that individual will be expected to join the process at this point. (For guidance in selecting a facilitator, see Step 4.)

Participants

The self-assessment process calls for roles to be assumed in six areas. Individuals may be involved in more than one way and, in smaller organizations, there is often significant overlap. Self-assessment makes real demands in terms of energy and time. Leadership must emphasize the importance of the process and support others' ability to balance ongoing work with self-assessment responsibilities.

Leadership Team

MEMBERS: Board chairman and chief executive officer or their equivalents in an all-volunteer organization. The chief executive is accountable for managing the process and is the primary liaison with the facilitator. The chairman is responsible for gaining the board's commitment to the self-assessment process and for presenting the final plan for board action.

ROLE: Oversee the entire self-assessment process:

- Gain commitment from the board and management.
- Lead the Assessment Team.
- Complete a Participant Workbook.
- Participate in customer research.
- Participate in a depth interview.
- Join in a retreat or group discussions.
- Review reports and approve final drafts.
- Confirm the plan for presentation to the board (as part of the Assessment Team).
- Present vision, mission, goals, and supporting budget for board approval (board chairman).
- Oversee development of objectives, action steps, and budget (chief executive).

TIME COMMITMENT: The Leadership Team confers frequently and meets with the Assessment Team a dozen or more times throughout the self-assessment process.

Assessment Team

MEMBERS: Board chairman, chief executive, and other members of the board and staff. The Assessment Team may be composed solely of the chairman and chief executive, but generally teams are larger. The exact number of members and the team's composition depends on the organization's size and management, as well as its decision-making philosophy.

ROLE: To assist the board chairman and chief executive officer in designing and carrying out the self-assessment process:

- Confirm self-assessment participants.
- Design the environmental scan, customer-research format, and depth interviews.

- Participate in conducting the environmental scan and customer research.
- Complete a Participant Workbook.
- Join in a retreat or group discussions.
- Review self-assessment reports and the plan.
- Draft a vision statement and revised mission statement if called for.
- Confirm the total plan for presentation to the board.

TIME COMMITMENT: The Assessment Team meets a dozen or more times throughout the self-assessment process.

Self-Assessment Participants

MEMBERS: Board members, a group of staff representing all levels of the organization, and customers, when possible and appropriate. In smaller organizations, most or all staff members, board members, and key volunteers may be involved.

ROLE: Review advance materials, complete a Participant Workbook, attend an orientation session, attend a retreat or two group discussions, and play one or more roles in customer research.

TIME COMMITMENT: Two to four hours reviewing advance materials and completing a Participant Workbook, a minimum of two four-hour discussions or a day-long retreat, and varying amounts of time participating in customer research.

Depth Interview Participants

MEMBERS: Board members, staff, and key volunteers whose insights are thought to be especially valuable or best gained through a depth interview.

ROLE: Complete a Participant Workbook, participate in an individual interview, and whenever possible, attend the retreat or group discussions.

TIME COMMITMENT: Two to four hours completing a Participant Workbook and a thirty-to-sixty-minute interview.

Objective, Action Step, and Budget Work Groups

MEMBERS: Staff and, in organizations where they play equivalent operating roles, volunteers, who will be responsible for meeting objectives and carrying out action steps. Specific staff members or volunteers are designated to lead groups that are developing action steps.

ROLE: Review self-assessment reports, gain a clear understanding of goals, develop draft objectives, action steps, and budgets for meeting them.

TIME COMMITMENT: One to three hours reading and review, a varying number of planning meetings.

Facilitation

MEMBERS: Individuals with excellent facilitating, interviewing, and writing abilities, whether from inside or outside the organization. It is cost-effective and builds skills to have an internal writer. (Resource 3 provides a helpful guide to effective facilitation; the topic is also discussed later in Step 4: Select a Facilitator and a Writer.)

ROLE: Can be as little as preparing for and facilitating a retreat or group discussions to as much as consulting throughout the process, participating in the environmental scan and customer research, conducting depth interviews, and assuming some of the writing responsibilities. This role may be shared by more than one person.

TIME COMMITMENT: Potentially significant, varies depending on the process design, the definition of the role, and whether responsibilities are shared.

Writing

MEMBERS: Individuals with requisite writing and reporting abilities, whether from inside or outside the organization.

ROLE: Development of reports and a plan. This role may be taken on by the facilitator, assigned to another person, or distributed as individual writing assignments. The writer's task is to synthesize what has been seen, heard, and decided upon and then to refine the copy and do the final edit, based on input and feedback from others.

TIME COMMITMENT: In addition to the time required for individual writing projects, people in this role must attend the retreat or group discussions and most Assessment Team meetings.

Process Design

The self-assessment process design details the specific steps the organization will complete, who is responsible for completing them, and by when. When thinking through process design, the board chairman and chief executive take into account the purpose for undertaking self-assessment, an overall time frame, the organization's structure, culture, and decision-making practices, and when and in what settings participants are most available.

Time Frame

Self-assessment should be completed in the shortest time possible without sacrificing proper attention to the process. A fast time line for a full organizational self-assessment is three to four months, and it is not uncommon for organizations to take a year. It is best to set an ambitious yet realistic time line and keep things moving. Otherwise, people lose interest or doubt the seriousness of the process.

Three Design Variables

Option A: Two Group Discussions vs. Option B: One Group Retreat

Holding two group discussions calls for an environmental scan in Phase One of the process and conducting customer research and depth interviews in Phase Two. Option A allows major self-assessment tasks to be spaced apart, can provide a greater range of opportunities for involvement than Option B, and gives more time to digest and consider self-assessment findings before final recommendations are developed.

Holding a retreat requires that the environmental scan, customer research, and depth interviews all be completed during Phase One. In this case, the Assessment Team works ahead to identify primary and supporting customers, conduct research and interviews, and report findings. Option B helps concentrate self-assessment into a shorter time period and is preferable when self-assessment participants are difficult to bring together, as in the case of national boards.

Conducting parallel sessions

For a variety of reasons, some organizations choose to separate the board and staff for a retreat or group discussions or to hold a number of self-assessment sessions, then combine input in one final report. This may be a pragmatic decision—the board meets only three or four times a year, and it is difficult to involve others at these times—or a feeling that more than one set of discussions will be most productive. Parallel sessions are often held when involving a very large number of self-assessment participants.

Whether to hold orientation sessions

Self-assessment discussions are designed as intensive, direction-setting and decision-making meetings. When feasible, orientation sessions on the overall process, roles, and expectations, as well as advance presentations of reports and findings, may enhance many individuals' readiness and ability to contribute.

To complete Step 1, the Leadership Team decides:

- What elements of the process are needed to meet the organization's purpose for self-assessment
- Who will be asked to participate and in what roles
- Whether to hold a retreat or two group discussions
- Whether to hold parallel sessions and, if so, how many
- Whether to hold orientation sessions
- How many Assessment Team meetings there will be (approximately) and when they will be held
- Who will facilitate and who will assume the writing responsibilities
- Whether to engage an outside facilitator at this point
- Who has lead responsibility; what deadlines for each step in the process will be
- What the budget for meetings and travel, as well as for a facilitator (if hired) or for other expenses, will be

STARS, Inc. is used throughout the Process Guide to illustrate comprehensive organizational self-assessment. STARS, Inc. is based on a real organization; only minor circumstances and details have been altered. STARS, Inc. preferred Design Option A: Two Group Discussions and decided to conduct parallel sessions with board and staff. The process began in mid July and is shown in Exhibit 1.

Exhibit 1

Sample Process Design for Comprehensive Organizational Self-Assessment for STARS, Inc.

Phase One: Preparing for Self-Assessment

Step	Who's Responsible	By When
1. Gain commitment from the board and management.	Board chairman, exec	Aug
2. Determine participants and process design.	Exec, board chairman, facilitator (?)	Aug
3. Form the Assessment Team.	Exec, board chairman	Sept

Board chairman and chief executive, Staff planner, 3 additional board members

Hold initial A-Team meeting and:

- Confirm participants, process design, time frame.
- Develop questions and process for environmental scan.
- Assign responsibility for gathering internal data.

Step	Who's Responsible	By When
4. Select a facilitator and a writer.	A-Team	Sept
5. Announce the process, invite participation, and confirm key dates.	Exec	Oct
6. Conduct environmental scan and gather internal data.	A-Team	Oct

Phase Two: Conducting the Self-Assessment Process

Step	Who's Responsible	By When
1. Orient participants to self-assessment process, present summary of environmental scan and internal data, distribute Workbooks, and confirm dates of parallel board and staff group discussions.	Exec, facilitator	Dec

Step	Who's Responsible	By When
2. Hold first group discussions with board and with staff.	Full board, exec, staff planner, all staff, facilitator	Dec
3. Complete report on first group discussions and distribute to full board and staff.	Writer (staff planner)	Jan
4. Hold A-Team meeting to review draft report on first group discussion, plan customer research, and confirm depth interview participants.	A-Team, facilitator	Jan
5. Conduct customer research.	Staff planner, others	Feb/Mar
6. Conduct depth interviews.	Facilitator	Feb/Mar
7. Complete draft customer-research and depth interview reports and distribute to A-Team.	Staff planner, exec	Mar
8. Gain comments on draft reports from A-Team members, revise as necessary, and distribute to board and staff.	Staff planner, exec	Mar
9. Hold second group discussion with board and with staff.	Board, exec, staff planner, all staff, facilitator	Apr
10. Prepare final report and distribute.	Staff planner, facilitator, exec	Apr

Phase Three: Complete and Implement the Plan

Step	Who's Responsible	By When
1. Hold two or more A-Team meetings to revise mission (if needed) and confirm goals and results.	A-Team	Apr
2. Design process for developing objectives, action steps, and budgets, make assignments, and hold orientation for work group leaders.	Exec	May
3. Develop draft objectives, action steps, and budgets.	Staff planner, exec, and work group leaders	May/June

Exhibit 1 (continued)

Step	Who's Responsible	By When
4. Hold A-Team meetings to:	A-Team, facilitator	June
• Review or suggest modifications to draft objectives, action steps, and budgets.		
• Decide on vision statement.		
• Discuss presentation to board.		
5. Finalize plan.	A-Team, facilitator	July
6. Hold A-Team meeting to:	Board chairman, exec	Aug
• Finalize how plan will be presented to the board.		
• Decide responsibility for appraisal.		
• Determine plan distribution once approved.		
7. Present mission, goals, and supporting budget to board for approval.		Sept
8. Distribute plan, confirm responsibilities and dates for initial appraisal.	Exec	Upon approval

STEP 3   Form the Assessment Team

It is often asked whether self-assessment is best conducted by a task force committed to long-range planning or marketing. There is a definite need for the self-assessment process to be led by a small group—people who have the commitment and the time—who will direct and do this specialized work. The Assessment Team steers the process and distills considerable findings and input into the final format and language of the plan. The Team designs the environmental scan and customer research, keeps others updated on progress, and develops a vision statement and revised mission statement if they are needed.

Although an Assessment Team has considerable responsibility, it does not and should not make the major decisions of the organization on its own. If decision making becomes isolated, even the best planners end up overlooking things that are crucial to a sound plan and to its successful implementation. When people across the organization are included, you build ownership and commitment. The basis for dispersed leadership is created within the planning process itself; each person is clear from the start on his or her contribution to performance. So the self-assessment process calls for both a small task force *and* broad participation.

The nucleus of the Assessment Team is the board chairman and chief executive. They are usually joined by additional members, but who those members should be differs, depending on the organization's structure, culture, and decision-making philosophy. There are a variety of opportunities for meaningful participation in self-assessment. The Assessment Team should be the right size and have the right players—with enough time—to effectively perform this central role.

At its initial meeting, the Assessment Team covers:

- Background on self-assessment and the organization's purpose in undertaking it
- Review, amendment, and confirmation of the process design
- Facilitator and writer selection or confirmation
- Preliminary discussion of the environmental scan and gathering internal data
- Preliminary discussion of customer research and depth interviews (if they are to be conducted in Phase One of the process)
- Next steps, assignments, and meeting dates

STEP 4   Select a facilitator and a writer

The facilitator

A great deal of work and struggle go into any true self-assessment; major decisions *should* be controversial. The self-assessment process asks, "What will *you* do to shape the future?" and pushes participants to expand their vision, tighten their focus, make difficult choices, and be accountable. To ensure that all opinions are heard, that no one goes off on a tangent, and that dissent remains constructive, a facilitator is recommended for a retreat or group discussions and other decision-making sessions.

Customer research conducted for this revised edition of the *Self-Assessment Tool* found that three-quarters of organizations used a designated facilitator for their process. Of those, 60 percent used someone from inside the organization, 36 percent engaged an outsider, and 4 percent had a combination of the two.

Here are four options for handling facilitation:

1. *Use an inside facilitator.* Using an inside facilitator—whether a board member, staff member, or current volunteer—saves the time and complexity of orienting an outsider to the organization. It gives one or more individuals the opportunity to exercise facilitation and interviewing skills, makes good use of the organization's existing resources, and may foster internal commitment to the process and resulting plan. It is best if neither the board chairman nor chief executive facilitates, as this limits the ability of these key individuals to fully participate. A facilitator must be objective and neutral throughout the process—a particular challenge for the insider who assumes this role.

2. *Hire an outside facilitator.* Engaging a qualified outside volunteer or paid consultant brings proven expertise to the role, frees everyone inside the organization to focus on other aspects of the process, and provides a catalyst to keep focused and on track. It is important that an outside facilitator be generally familiar with social sector organizations and a quick study with regard to an institution's background and culture. Bringing in an outside facilitator is one way of demonstrating commitment to self-assessment and, because of the outsider's natural neutrality, participants may find it easier to be frank.

3. *Designate no one as facilitator.* Completing self-assessment without using a facilitator requires an extremely clear process design, consistent follow-up on each assigned responsibility, and excellent teamwork. This option is most effective for organizations with experience or a strong commitment to developing shared skills in process and meeting management. Without a facilitator, it is especially important that groups have ground rules for their work and guard against unfocused discussion, the vocal individual who dominates, and dissent that may slip into conflict.

4. *Use both inside and outside facilitators.* Combining inside and outside facilitators adds complexity to managing the role but is also an opportunity to have the best of both worlds. If the process design that is selected calls for a large number of group sessions or depth interviews—and particularly if the organization is geographically dispersed—having an outside facilitator train and direct one or more insiders may be advantageous.

Effective facilitation can go a long way toward bringing out the best in all members of a group (see Resource 2 for a detailed discussion). Because self-assessment calls for broad contribution and encourages dissent, discussion must be handled well so it does not wander or degenerate into harmful conflict. Facilitators, therefore, should be carefully selected for their skill and objectivity. A facilitator may also help design the self-assessment process, take on some writing responsibilities, and play a role in conducting the environmental scan and customer research. Most self-assessment process designs call for the facilitator to conduct depth interviews.

The selection of inside facilitators is usually based on knowledge and prior experience of candidates' skills. *When selecting an outsider, the Assessment Team:*

- Conducts preliminary screening
- Requests written proposals (from potential paid consultants)
- Conducts initial interviews
- Checks references
- Conducts final interviews and makes a selection

The writer

There are five to seven writing projects in the self-assessment process. A sample of each is provided in upcoming chapters. The writing projects are:

1. Findings from the environmental scan and summary of internal data.
2. Summary of the first group discussion. (This summary is omitted when following Design Option B: Hold a Group Retreat.)
3. Customer research findings.
4. Depth interview findings.
5. Final report.
6. Vision statement and revised mission statement.
7. The plan.

These writing projects build understanding of the process and ownership of its findings. Therefore, the more writing that can be done inside the organization, the better. The writing role, like facilitation, can be handled in more than one fashion. Options include the following:

1. *Make writing one inside person's responsibility.* A good choice when there is an individual inside the organization with good writing ability, a strong interest in the assignment, and sufficient time.

2. *Make writing one outside person's responsibility.* There are cases when assigning writing responsibilities to a well-qualified outsider is appropriate. It saves staff time and ensures continuity and a consistent level of quality.

3. *Assign different writing projects to individuals or small teams.* Distributing writing projects is often the best approach. In this way time commitments, quality considerations, and ownership can all be balanced.

When choosing writers, take into account previous experience with similar projects and, whenever possible, review samples of past work. Self-assessment writing projects may certainly be viewed as opportunities for people inside the organization to develop skills. Draft self-assessment reports and plans are subject to input and feedback from the Assessment Team and should be edited for their accuracy and objectivity. Facilitators can also be helpful in an editorial role. The leadership team approves final drafts of reports and the final plan.

STEP 5   Announce the process, invite participation, and confirm key dates

Everyone who works with the organization should be informed that self-assessment is being undertaken. Such an announcement includes:

- The organization's purpose for undertaking self-assessment
- An introduction to the self-assessment process and Peter Drucker's Five Most Important Questions
- A summary of the process design
- Information regarding opportunities to participate, with key dates
- Introductions, as appropriate, of facilitators and writers

General announcements can be made via routine communications such as newsletters and e-mail or at regularly scheduled meetings. In addition, direct invitations are given to those being asked to fill out Participant Workbooks and to participate in group discussions, a retreat, or depth interviews. These invitations include detailed information about member roles and time commitments, give sufficient advance notice of meeting dates, and generally require formal RSVPs (with a good amount of follow-up) to confirm participation.

The timing for announcing the process and inviting participation depends on how long the environmental scan—and possible up-front customer research and depth interviews—are to take. If this portion of the process is lengthy, a general announcement at the very beginning may be followed with invitations to participate some time later.

Self-assessment leads to a plan that will have an impact throughout the organization. To build understanding, initial announcements and explanations should be the first of regular progress reports and briefings throughout the process.

STEP 6   Conduct an environmental scan and gather internal data

Through an environmental scan, key issues and trends can be discovered, as well as their implications in the environment that are likely to affect the organization in its future work. This information is used to orient self-assessment participants on the context in which the mission is to be carried out. Look outside the organization and gather pertinent information regarding:

1. Changing demographics of current and potential customer groups
2. Evolving community issues and conditions the organization might address
3. Relevant cultural or social trends
4. Trends in the economy or funding environment
5. Politics, legislation, or regulation that affects the organization and those it serves
6. Competition
7. New technologies, models, or methods

In addition to the environmental scan, internal data are gathered and summarized to orient participants to the history and present status of the organization. This may include a copy of the mission statement and:

- A historical summary
- Customer or member demographics
- Services delivered
- Bottom-line results
- Other measures of organizational performance
- An organizational chart
- Financial data
- Publications
- An annual report
- Other communication tools that provide background and insight into the organization

The Assessment Team designs the environmental scan and the scope of internal data, possibly with guidance from the facilitator or a research consultant. The chief executive is responsible for overseeing the scan and data gathering. Specific tasks may be assigned to staff, board members, volunteers, or paid consultants.

Design the environmental scan

The scope of an environmental scan differs with each self-assessment process. Some are full-scale projects in and of themselves and may require months to complete. Others are narrowly focused and much shorter term. It is best for the Assessment Team to begin with a wish list of all the questions to be answered and all the scanning techniques that might be employed. Then rank the items on the list, address questions of feasibility, and decide what *can* be done to gain the most critical information.

To design the environmental scan, the Assessment Team does the following:

- Determines as specifically as possible the areas the environmental scan is to address.
- Identifies information already available within the organization that can be used in the scan.
- Identifies outside sources for information that already exists.
- Considers whether to interview a group of "key informants." Such interviewees may include community leaders, elected officials, heads of other organizations with a related mission, funders, and others with valuable insight or expertise. (Conducting one or more key informant interviews is an excellent way to involve self-assessment participants in the environmental scan and, in some cases, is also a form of customer research.)
- Decides if the organization will conduct surveys, opinion polls, focus groups, or other forms of original research.
- Develops a work plan for obtaining and organizing information and makes assignments.

Environmental scan information can be obtained from a great variety of sources. Local governmental units, United Ways, universities, chambers of commerce, and research institutions are frequent providers of free or low-cost information, as are numerous Web sites and print and broadcast media. Discipline-specific institutes, associations, coalitions, and professional organizations (for example, American Association of Museums, Girl Scouts of the U.S.A., National Institutes of Health, National Council of Churches of Christ in the U.S.A., Children's Defense Fund) provide data within specific social sector fields. Exhibit 2 is a list of organizations that report trends pertinent to a wide range of social sector organizations on a national and international scale. Please check the Drucker Foundation Web site (www.pfdf.org) for updates to this list.

Exhibit 2

Sources for Environmental Scan Information

American Association of Fund-Raising Counsel and the *AAFRC Trust for Philanthropy* is a membership organization made up of firms throughout North America providing fundraising consultation and program services to nonprofit organizations. The AAFRC Trust for Philanthropy publishes *GIVING USA,* an annual report often sourced by major media in coverage of philanthropy. Additional specialized reports on giving trends are also available. Costs vary.

> AAFRC and AAFRC Trust for Philanthropy
> 25 W. 42nd Street
> New York, NY 10036
> Phone: (212) 354-5799
> (888) 544-8464 (toll free to order reports)
> Fax: (412) 741-0609 (to order reports)
> E-mail: aafrc@compuserve.com
> Web address: www.aafrc.org

The Conference Board is the world's leading business membership and research organization, connecting senior executives from more than 2,300 enterprises in over sixty nations. The Conference Board produces the *Consumer Confidence Index* and *Leading Economic Indicators,* as well as a host of reports and white papers on key environmental trends. Detailed information on publications is available on their Web site.

> The Conference Board
> 845 Third Avenue
> New York, NY 10022-6679
> Phone: (212) 759-0900
> Fax: (212) 980-7014
> E-mail: info@conference-board.org
> Web address: www.conference-board.org

The Foundation Center is an information clearinghouse that fosters public understanding of the foundation field by collecting, organizing, analyzing, and disseminating information on foundations, corporate giving, and related subjects. Access to the latest research findings on trends in giving and other key data is available through the Center's Web site, five Foundation Center libraries, and more than two hundred cooperating collections across the United States.

> The Foundation Center
> 79 Fifth Avenue
> New York, NY 10003-3076
> Phone: (212) 620-4230

Exhibit 2 (continued)

(800) 424-9836
Fax: (212) 807-3677
E-mail: library@fdncenter.org
Web address: http://fdncenter.org

Girl Scouts of the U.S.A., with over three million members, is dedicated to the purpose of inspiring girls with the highest ideals of character, conduct, patriotism, and service that they may become happy and resourceful citizens. Each year the organization produces an Environmental Scanning Report covering demography, economy, education, environment and energy, government and legislation, science and technology, and values and lifestyles. Copies are available at a modest cost.

Girl Scouts of the U.S.A.
420 Fifth Avenue
New York, NY 10018-2798
Phone: (800) 223-0624
Fax: (212) 852-6510
E-mail: admin@gsusa.org
Web address: http://www.gsusa.org

Graphic, Visualization & Usability Center at Georgia Institute of Technology pursues the vision of making computers accessible to and usable for every individual. Since 1994, the Center has conducted the World Wide Web User Survey, which includes general demographics, technology demographics, Web and Internet usage, electronic commerce, trends, and analysis. The survey is updated every six months, is available on-line, and costs $50.00.

GVU Center
Georgia Institute of Technology
College of Computing Building
Atlanta, GA 30332-0280
Phone: (404) 894-4488
Fax: (404) 894-0673
Web address: www.gvu.gatech.edu

INDEPENDENT SECTOR is a coalition of more than eight hundred foundation, corporate, and voluntary organization members with national interest and impact in philanthropy and voluntary action. Published reports include "Giving and Volunteering in the United States," "Giving and Volunteering Among Teenagers," "Nonprofit Almanac," which focuses on trends and statistics, and many others. Publication prices vary.

INDEPENDENT SECTOR
1828 L Street NW
Washington, DC 20036

Phone: (202) 223-8100
(800) 575-2666 (document on request)
(301) 490-3229 (publication orders)
Fax: (202) 416-0580
E-mail: info@indepsec.org
Web address: www.indepsec.org

Morgan Quitno Press is an independent research and publishing company that specializes in reference books and reports that compare states and cities in key areas. The four primary ranking reference books are *State Rankings, Health Care State Rankings, Crime State Rankings,* and *City Crime Rankings. State Rankings* features hundreds of categories ranging from agriculture to health, transportation, crime, and social welfare. Prices are in the $40.00 range per book.

Morgan Quitno Press
P.O. Box 1656
Lawrence, KS 66044-8656
Phone: (785) 841-3534
(800) 457-0742
Fax: (785) 841-3538
E-mail: mqpn@midusa.net
Web address: http://www.morganquitno.com

National Opinion Research Center (NORC) is a nonprofit organization affiliated with the University of Chicago that conducts survey research in the public interest. The GSS (General Social Survey) is a regular, ongoing, omnibus personal interview survey of U.S. households. Survey topics include national spending priorities, drinking behavior, drug use, sexual behaviors, crime and punishment, race relations, quality of life, confidence in institutions, and membership in voluntary associations. The GSS is available on NORC's Web site.

NORC
3050 Finley Road
Downers Grove, IL 60515
Phone: (630) 434-1400
Fax: (630) 434-1405
E-mail: norcinfo@norcmail.uchicago.edu
Web address: www.norc.uchicago.edu

National Society of Fund Raising Executives (NSFRE) is committed to international cooperation and exchange of knowledge, techniques, and education among fundraising executives. NSFRE Resource Center services are available to members free of charge. Nonmember fees are based on the number of topics for which information is provided.

Exhibit 2 (continued)

The NSFRE Fund Raising Resource Center
National Society of Fund Raising Executives
1101 King Street, Suite 700
Alexandria, VA 22314-2967
Phone: (800) 688-3463
(703) 684-0410
Fax: (703) 684-0540
E-mail: resctr@nsfre.org
Web address: www.nsfre.org

U.S. Census Bureau is the official statistic keeper for the United States and has a wealth of social, demographic, and economic information. The World Wide Web posts a number of relevant e-mail addresses and has made access to the Census Bureau's "preeminent collection of timely, relevant, and quality data" much easier and more complete than ever before. The Web site is complex and requires considerable navigation.

U.S. Census Bureau
1st and Constitution Avenue NE
Silver Springs, MD 20907
Phone: (301) 457-1722
(800) 272-4250
E-mail: webmaster@census.gov
Web address: www.census.gov

Report of findings from the environmental scan

As the scan is completed, the Assessment Team holds one or more meetings to review information and guide the writer in identifying the strongest points that help to paint a picture of the organization's context. Although a tremendous amount of information may have been gathered and reviewed, the brief report:

- States only *key findings*—facts, trends, implications, and points of interest that highlight challenges and opportunities in the organization's operating environment.
- Supports key findings with bullet points or short quotes summarizing the most relevant information.
- Includes an appendix with sources of information.

There are many ways to organize the report. Three common formats are:

1. *Question and answer:* You pose the questions you want the scan to answer and respond to them.
2. *Categories:* You report findings in each of the seven categories listed in Phase One, Step 6.
3. *Key themes:* You report the important themes that emerged through the scan.

A sample report is provided in Exhibit 3. A summary of internal data accompanies the environmental scan report. Copies of lengthier environmental scan and internal source materials may be prepared for self-assessment participants who request them.

To complete this step, the Assessment Team:

- Meets to review environmental scan information and internal data.
- Works with the writer to identify key findings for the report.
- Reviews a draft report of findings and summary of internal data.
- Gains the chief executive's approval of final drafts.
- Plans orientation sessions.

  When feasible, organizations hold orientation sessions to review environmental scan findings and internal data prior to a retreat or first group discussion. Such advance sessions deepen the understanding gained from written reports.

- Prepares a presentation for the orientation sessions, first group discussion, or retreat.

  One or more individuals are assigned to develop and present an overview of findings and respond to questions.

Exhibit 3

Sample Internal Data Summary and Environmental Scan Report for STARS, Inc.

Internal Data Summary

STARS, Inc. (Southwest Training and Retraining Services) is a fifteen-year-old organization serving fourteen rural counties with the mission: *to provide employment, training, and related services to eligible participants in the service area so that those persons will be able to support themselves and to reenter the economic mainstream of the southwest region.*

The organization operates nine programs with a staff of twenty-five and a budget of $5 million, which is derived almost exclusively from federal and state contracts and project grants. The organization does not carry a deficit, but there are no cash reserves. In the past year, 3,888 individuals were served, all either economically disadvantaged (70 percent) or permanently laid off through no fault of their own (30 percent). Eighty percent of those served were adults, and 20 percent were youth. Forty percent of all those served were receiving welfare. In every program, STARS exceeded federal performance standards for employment rates, retention up to thirteen weeks following job placement, weekly earnings, and "youth employability enhancement."

STARS faces a volatile and challenging environment. Staff and board are concerned about upheaval in traditional government funding, rapidly changing employment patterns, and shifting community demographics. The STARS, Inc. board determines the need to step back from "business as usual" and develop a focused three-year plan for the organization.

Environmental Scan Report

A. Decreasing population base
   - 11.9 percent decrease from 1980–1990 in fourteen-county service area
   - 1980s decrease due, in part, to farm crisis resulting in loss of whole families with children, many of whom would have entered area labor force
   - Population predicted to continue declining but at slower pace
B. "Graying" population
   - 35–40 percent of service area population over fifty, compared to 16 percent in nearest large metropolitan area
   - Graying trend expected to continue in rural areas as fewer young people move in and older residents "age in place"

C. Increased diversity
- Although population is 96 percent white, 4 percent nonwhite population is double that of a decade ago
- One high-profile initiative to recruit entry-level workers from urban area resulted in public meetings to examine related wage, housing, and potential welfare issues associated with attracting low-income, unskilled workers to region
- Recent outplacement work in one area factory closing necessitated translators for seven different non-English-speaking populations

D. Strong economic indicators but low minimum wage
- Unemployment figures for service area "lowest in memory"
- State officials reporting "strongest economy in twenty-five years"
- Manufacturing sector employers reporting inability to keep pace with orders
- Median wage for new jobs in service area is $6.50 per hour

E. More participants with multiple barriers to employment
- Strong economy has enabled those with competitive skills to gain employment independently
- Staff caseloads show increased number of participants needing intensive help to build basic employment skills as well as need for ongoing supporting services to meet working family needs based on income from entry-wage jobs

F. Important unmet needs outside the scope of "eligible participants"
- Government guidelines often judge those in entry-level jobs ineligible for services that may result in moving up to higher-paying positions
- In past eighteen months, staff phone logs indicate up to 20 percent increase in requests for service from "non-eligible" residents of area, mostly in regard to career assessment, training, help with movement to higher-paying positions, and women reentering the paid workforce

G. Increasing need for technologically skilled workers
- Global shift to "knowledge society" being felt in local economy, especially with regard to better-paying positions
- Employers report need for much more rapid retraining options than those available through traditional vocational school programs

H. Emerging emphasis on school-to-work transition
- Federal school-to-work legislation requires curricula developed with area employers that prepares students to exercise option to directly enter the workforce upon high school graduation
- Federal funding in support of school-to-work transition is flowing directly to school systems

Exhibit 3 (continued)

I. Decreased federal funding for job training programs
  - 30 percent decrease in available funding from 1994 to 1996 after almost eight years of stable federal funding at higher levels
  - Former funding level not expected to be restored

J. State role funding employment services in flux
  - Block grant funding, which may increase state resources, has not yet materialized
  - State policies are resulting in consolidation of employment-related funding, but new systems are not in place and levels and channels of funding are not yet predictable

K. Welfare reform
  - Counties will clearly have increased role and may have increased resources—will require individual coordination with all fourteen counties in service area rather than former more centralized federal model
  - Expectation will be for closer system integration with county workers, but policies and procedures not yet in place
  - Expectation is increased number of program participants who must gain employment by clear deadlines; flow of funding to support expanded services is in question
  - Expectation is that "welfare reform" participants will largely fit "low-skilled, low-functioning, multiple barriers to employment" profile

L. Need for increased collaboration
  - The practical result of many of the issues listed is the need for partnerships with government systems and community agencies to support entry-level and transitional workers with training as well as child care, transportation, and other services to enhance job-readiness and career advancement potential
  - Educational institutions and employers need employment services partners to carry out their mandates and address the rapidly shifting skill sets required of existing and new employees in the changing economy

Sources of information for environmental scan:

1. Census data
2. State Department of Economic Security Research and Statistics
3. New participant inquiries and internal case management data
4. STARS, Inc. regional survey of welfare recipients on demographics, work experience, work interests, and employment-related basic skills and personal support systems

5. STARS, Inc. regional survey of employers on desired workforce profiles, employ-ment opportunities, working family support systems, and attitudes in regard to employment of welfare recipients

6. Related news reports and articles

7. Historical review of budget and funding patterns

8. Staff and board member reports from area task forces, meetings with govern-ment officials, and participation in formal cross-sector collaborations

Conducting the Self-Assessment Process

Phase Two brings self-assessment to life for many more participants inside your organization, and customer research takes you *outside* to gain direct knowledge from your customers of what they value. The voice of the customer then becomes an integral part of your organization's decision making. In Phase Two, Participant Workbooks, depth interviews, and facilitated discussions guide self-assessment participants through Peter Drucker's five questions. A final report summarizes what has been learned on the journey thus far.

The five steps in Phase Two are:

1. Orient participants; distribute environmental scan summary report, internal data, and the Participant Workbook.
2. Hold group discussion on the first three Drucker questions or hold a group retreat.
3. Conduct customer research and depth interviews.*
4. Hold group discussion on the fourth and fifth Drucker questions.**
5. Prepare and distribute final report.

*Conducted during Phase One when holding a group retreat.
**First and second group discussions are combined when holding a group retreat.

Overview of Phase Two

■ Step 1: Orient participants; distribute internal data, environmental scan summary report, and the Participant Workbook

The Assessment Team orients self-assessment participants and directs their preparations for a first group discussion or retreat. Orientation takes place either in meetings or by way of distributed materials (or both).

■ Step 2: Hold group discussion on the first three Drucker questions or hold a group retreat

The overriding purpose of self-assessment group discussions or a retreat is to build common knowledge and commitment to the organization's mission, goals, and results. This happens through an exchange of thought and opinion in which constructive dissent is encouraged. The Assessment Team and facilitator develop an agenda and tend to the details essential to effective meetings. A summary report is developed and distributed.

■ Step 3: Conduct customer research and depth interviews

Customer research produces firsthand information on customers' needs, wants, and aspirations—what they value. In Step 3, research produces the information needed from customers and brings powerful statements of what customers value into the self-assessment process. Depth interviews enrich the self-assessment process by highlighting responses to Peter Drucker's questions from a select group of individuals inside the organization. A customer-research and depth interview report is developed and distributed.

■ Step 4: Hold group discussion on the fourth and fifth Drucker questions

The Assessment Team and facilitator develop an agenda and prepare the details of the meeting. A briefing on customer-research and depth interview findings may occur before or during this group discussion. This step may be combined with Step 2 as a retreat.

Step 5: Prepare and distribute final report

Phase Two concludes with a final report of participants' conclusions to this point in the self-assessment process.

Detailed Steps

STEP 1   Orient participants; distribute internal data, environmental scan summary report, and the Participant Workbook

The self-assessment process now moves into its second phase, as the Assessment Team orients self-assessment participants and helps prepare them to take part in group discussions or a retreat. Orientation takes place by way of distributed materials, in meetings, or both.

The Assessment Team prepares a packet of orientation materials including:

1. A cover memo with a general update and instructions, assignments to complete in the Participant Workbook, and reminders of the purpose and dates for upcoming meetings.
2. Design Option A: Internal data and the environmental scan report—for a first group discussion.

   Design Option B: Internal data, the environmental scan report, customer-research and depth interview reports—for a retreat.
3. An agenda for the first group discussion or retreat (see next step).
4. A copy of the Participant Workbook.

   Self-assessment participants receive a general update and are asked to:

- Review reports on environment and internal data, and any additional background materials.
- Read through the entire Participant Workbook.
- Respond to assigned worksheets before attending a first group discussion or retreat.

  If you are holding two group discussions, assign the first *three* Drucker questions, Worksheets 1–8. (Worksheet 9 is used in the first group discussion.)

  If you are holding a retreat, assign all *five* Drucker questions, Worksheets 1–16. (Worksheet 9 is omitted.)

Whenever feasible, orientation sessions are strongly encouraged. These advance opportunities to hear, discuss, and digest information contribute a great deal to successful retreats and group discussions. In some instances, the Assessment Team reaches out with one-to-one briefings for key board members and others who may not be able to attend group sessions.

STEP 2   Hold group discussion on the first three Drucker questions or hold a group retreat

▓ Tend to detail

Seeing to logistics, comforts, assignments, and other effective meeting preparations sets the stage for productive discussion. *Details for the Assessment Team to tend to include:*

- Finding a convenient and comfortable location
- Acquiring and testing equipment if audio recordings of the sessions will be made
- Assigning and preparing presentation of reports
- Preparing or collecting any additional materials to be distributed at the sessions
- Selecting people to introduce the sessions
- Finalizing the agenda with the facilitator
- Preparing a written agenda for participants
- Confirming the form and timing of reports expected from the writer
- Acquiring flip charts, overhead projectors, and other audiovisual aids
- Purchasing refreshments and supplies such as pads and pens
- Confirming attendance

In Exhibit 4, sample agendas (both in outline and in more detail) are shown for a first group discussion and then for a retreat.

Note: Many organizations find it valuable to extend group discussions or a retreat when time permits. Expanded agendas may:
- Allow for lengthier exchanges of views
- Provide greater opportunities to delve into and resolve complex issues
- Shift refinement of some self-assessment decisions from the Assessment Team to the larger participant group
- Include additional team-building and educational exercises
- Add social time
- Incorporate other activities or adaptations

Exhibit 4

Sample Agendas for a First Group Discussion and for a Retreat

Option A—First Group Discussion

Sample Objectives and Agenda

Objectives

1. Assess the mission and determine whether it needs to be revisited.
2. Identify the organization's most significant challenges and opportunities.
3. Identify the primary and supporting customers, how they will change, and what the organization believes they value.
4. Outline what needs to be learned from customers.
5. Gain commitments to participate in customer research.

Agenda

I. Extend welcome; give introductions and overview; discuss ground rules.
II. Review the mission, environmental scan, and internal data (Worksheet 1).
III. Identify the most significant challenges and opportunities (Worksheets 2 and 3).
IV. Refreshment break
V. Identify the primary customers, how they will change, what the organization believes they value (Worksheets 5, 6, and 7).
VI. Identify the supporting customers, how they will change, what the organization believes they value; discuss potential new customers or customers to stop serving (Worksheets 5, 6, and 7).
VII. Stretch break
VIII. Ask the question, What knowledge should be gained from customers? (Worksheet 8).
IX. Gain commitment to participate in customer research (Worksheet 9).
X. Ask the question, Does the mission need to be revisited? (Worksheet 4).
XI. Conduct discussion about next steps; adjourn.

Total session time: 4 hours

Exhibit 4 (continued)

First Group Discussion: Sample Annotated Agenda

Total time: 4 hours

I.	10 min.	Give welcome, introductions, overview.

One or more members of the Assessment Team handles:

- General welcome
- Introduction of participants
- Overview of the self-assessment process
- Confirmation of decision-making protocols
- Discussion of purpose of the session and agenda overview
- Introduction of writer and facilitator

	10 min.	Set the ground rules.

The facilitator leads an exercise in which participants suggest a set of points all agree will encourage constructive dissent and help ensure the most productive session. The facilitator also confirms his or her role with the group.

II.	15 min.	Review the mission.

The facilitator asks participants to join with two or three others near them and spend ten minutes sharing responses to Worksheet 1. Then, following this warm-up, participants are invited to briefly recap responses and impressions in the large group.

	20 min.	Review the environmental scan and internal data.

Environmental scan findings and internal data are presented by one or more members of the Assessment Team, followed by a question-and-answer period.

III.	15 min.	Identify the most significant challenges and opportunities.

The facilitator places participants in groups of six to eight people. Half the groups are assigned the category "challenges"; the other half address "opportunities." Each small group is supplied with flip chart paper, asked to refer to Worksheets 2 or 3, and given ten minutes to list what group members see as the most significant challenges and opportunities for the organization.

	20 min.	Flip charts are posted for the large group to view.

The facilitator invites additions, then completes this portion with a poll to identify the challenges and opportunities that are seen as most significant. Participants are given three to five "votes" in each of the two categories. The facilitator tallies votes on the flip charts and leads a short discussion.

IV.	10 min.	Refreshment break

V.	30 min.	Identify primary customers and discuss how they will change.

The facilitator begins by noting that even though participants completed Worksheet 4 in their advance preparation, the group will discuss Worksheet 4 later in the session. The facilitator directs participants to Worksheet 5, elicits answers to the question, Who is our primary customer? and strives for a consensus on one primary customer group. The facilitator then directs participants to Worksheet 6, calls for and records highlights of their responses, then draws out overall conclusions on the question, Will our primary customers change?

Note: "Who is our customer?" can produce significant discussion and difference of opinion. The facilitator should adjust the agenda to ensure that there is adequate time on this question; if necessary, make time to revisit it in the second group discussion.

	20 min.	Ask what the organization believes its primary customers value.

Participants turn to Worksheet 7, and the facilitator calls for, records, and posts the group's beliefs on what the primary customer values. A discussion follows in which participants identify areas of agreement and disagreement in the group's responses.

VI.	30 min.	Identify supporting customers and discuss how they will change.

The facilitator directs participants back to Worksheet 5 and records the group's responses to the question, Who are your supporting customers? Participants are then placed in small groups, assigned one or more supporting customers, asked to refer to Worksheet 6, and given fifteen minutes to discuss and record highlights of their responses to the seven worksheet sections. This portion concludes with brief verbal reports to the large group and collecting what has been recorded in the small groups for use by the writer. Small groups stay together for the next exercise.

	20 min.	Ask what supporting customers value.

Continuing with their assigned supporting customers, small groups refer to Worksheet 7 and discuss and record what they believe supporting customers value. This portion also concludes with brief verbal reports and the collection of recorded comments.

VII.	5 min.	Stretch break

VIII.	10 min.	Determine what needs to be learned from customers.

In the large group, the facilitator calls for a few examples of what participants want to learn directly from primary and supporting customers. Then, with half the group addressing primary customers and the other half addressing supporting customers, participants are asked to write a list of what they would like to learn and to hand it in.

Exhibit 4 (continued)

IX. 5 min. Affirm commitment to participate in customer research.

Copies of Worksheet 9 are handed out, possible types of customer research are quickly noted, and participants are asked to fill out the copy, sign their name at the bottom, and hand it in.

X. 15 min. Ask whether the mission needs to be revisited.

The facilitator directs participants to Worksheet 4 and gives a few moments for participants to review their responses in light of discussion to this point. The facilitator tells participants they are free to modify their original response, then asks for a show of hands on the three possible answers to the question, Should the mission be revisited? The facilitator asks for a group conclusion. If the answer is "Not at all," the facilitator calls for and records reasons for keeping the mission as it stands. If the answer is "To some extent" or "Yes, absolutely," the facilitator asks for brief comments and notes that participants will continue to consider what the mission should be as the group works through the fourth and fifth Drucker questions. The mission is revisited in the second group discussion.

XI. 5 min. Discuss next steps; adjourn.

The facilitator invites closing comments, then turns the session back to a member of the Assessment Team to review next steps regarding customer research, depth interviews, and the second group discussion. The board chairman or chief executive thanks participants and adjourns the meeting.

Option B—Retreat

Sample Objectives and Agenda

Objectives

1. Revisit the mission and, if needed, propose change.
2. Identify most significant challenges and opportunities.
3. Confirm definitions of the primary and supporting customers, how they will change, and what they value.
4. Outline what results for the organization should be.
5. Identify what must be strengthened, abandoned, or analyzed.
6. Recommend goals for the plan.

Agenda

I. Extend welcome; make introductions; discuss overview and ground rules.
II. Review the current mission (Worksheet 1).
III. Review the environmental scan, internal data, depth interview and customer-research findings.
IV. Identify the most significant challenges and opportunities (Worksheets 2 and 3).
V. Refreshment break
VI. Confirm the primary and supporting customers, how they will change, what they value, potential new customers, and customers to stop serving (Worksheets 5, 6, and 7).
VII. Meal break
VIII. Ask the question, Have we been successful? (Worksheets 10 and 11).
IX. Outline results (Worksheet 12).
X. Identify what must be strengthened, abandoned, or analyzed (Worksheet 13).
XI. Refreshment break
XII. Revisit the mission (Worksheets 4 and 14).
XIII. Recommend goals (Worksheet 15).
XIV. Review the next steps.
XV. Conduct the closing.

7 hours

Exhibit 4 (continued)

Group Retreat: Sample Annotated Agenda

Total time: 7 hours

I. 10 min. Give welcome, introductions, overview.

One or more members of the Assessment Team handles:
  * General welcome
  * Introduction of participants
  * Overview of the self-assessment process
  * Confirmation of decision-making protocols
  * Discussion of purpose of the session, agenda overview, use of information from the environmental scan, internal data, depth interviews, and customer research
  * Introduction of writer and facilitator

10 min. Set the ground rules.

The facilitator leads an exercise in which participants suggest a set of points all agree will encourage constructive dissent and help ensure the most productive session. The facilitator also confirms his or her role with the group.

II. 15 min. Review the mission.

The facilitator asks participants to join with two or three others near them and spend ten minutes sharing responses to Worksheet 1. Then, following this warm-up, participants are invited to briefly recap responses and impressions in the large group.

III. 35 min. Review the findings from the environmental scan, internal data, depth interviews, and customer research.

Internal data and environmental scan, depth interview, and customer-research findings are presented by one or members of the Assessment Team, followed by a question-and-answer period.

IV. 25 min. Identify the most significant challenges and opportunities.

The facilitator places participants in groups of six to eight people. Half the groups are assigned the category "challenges"; the other half address "opportunities." Each small group is supplied with flip chart paper and asked to refer to environmental scan and depth interview findings, as well as participants' responses to Worksheets 2 or 3. Groups are given ten minutes to list what participants see as the most significant challenges and opportunities for the organization.

20 min. Flip charts are posted for the large group to view.

The facilitator invites additions, then completes this portion with a poll to identify the challenges and opportunities that are seen as most significant. Participants are given three to five "votes" in each of the two categories. The facilitator tallies votes on the flip charts and leads a short discussion.

V.	10 min.	Refreshment break

VI.   15 min.   Confirm primary and supporting customers.

The Assessment Team has pre-identified primary and supporting customers for the purpose of customer research. A member of the Assessment Team presents these definitions and briefly recaps how they were arrived at. The facilitator leads a group discussion to confirm working definitions of primary and supporting customers to be used for the remainder of the session.

    25 min.   Confirm how primary customers will change and what they value.

The facilitator directs participants to Worksheets 6 and 7 and gives five minutes to review responses in light of environmental scan and customer-research findings. In a large-group discussion, the facilitator seeks confirmation of how primary customers will change and what they value. This portion concludes with a short group reflection on how these conclusions differ from prior beliefs.
    Note: "Who is our customer?" can produce significant discussion and difference of opinion. The facilitator should adjust the agenda to ensure that adequate time is spent on this question.

    30 min.   Confirm how supporting customers will change and what they value.

The facilitator divides participants into small groups, assigns each group one or more supporting customers, reminds participants to refer to Worksheets 6 and 7, and gives fifteen minutes to confirm, in light of environmental scan and customer-research findings, how supporting customers will change and what they value. Brief verbal reports are given in the large group, and what has been recorded in the small groups is collected for use by the writer.

VII.   30 min.   Meal break

VIII.   20 min.   Discussion: Have we been successful?

The facilitator directs participants to Worksheets 10 and 11 and gives a few moments to discuss responses informally in pairs or small groups. The facilitator leads a large-group discussion to confirm the organization's current definition of results, then gains the group's response to the question, Have we been successful? and highlights with which customers there are greater and lesser degrees of success.

IX.   40 min.   Outline results.

At this point in the retreat, a change of pace is in order. Here is a suggested exercise: The facilitator reminds participants that the organization's results are in changed lives, then asks that everyone have paper and pen ready. The facilitator leads a short guided imagery in which participants are asked to imagine the organization

Exhibit 4 (continued)

has been chosen to receive a Presidential Citation for Excellence, which will be announced during the State of the Union Address. Seated as special guests in the Congressional Gallery, participants hear the president say, "I wish to cite [your organization] as an example to the nation in changing lives. I am certainly inspired by the overall performance of [your organization]. Let me share how lives have been changed. . . ." At this point, the facilitator tells participants they have two minutes to complete the president's thoughts and asks them to begin writing immediately.

The facilitator asks each participant in turn to contribute one result they thought of and records responses on a flip chart until all potential results have been suggested.

The facilitator completes this portion by asking for the group's judgment of what results should be. What is realistic, yet ambitious? What are the best results that people really believe could be achieved?

X.	35 min.	Identify what must be strengthened, abandoned, or analyzed.

The facilitator places participants into four or five small groups and asks that they be mindful of discussion to this point as they complete their next assignment. Groups are then directed to Worksheet 13 and given fifteen minutes to agree on "candidates" for strengthening, abandonment, or analysis, as well as internal systems that should be assessed; then they are to write them on a piece of flip chart paper and post it. The large group is then given ten minutes to make a tour of the flip charts and write check marks next to the posted candidates with which they agree. The facilitator concludes this portion with discussion to confirm the group's priorities for potential strengthening, abandonment, analysis, and further assessment.

XI.	15 min.	Refreshment break
XII.	30 min.	Ask whether the mission should be changed.

The facilitator directs participants to Worksheet 14 and gives a moment for participants to review their response. The facilitator tells participants they are free to modify their original response, then asks for a show of hands on whether the mission should be changed. The facilitator asks for a group conclusion.

- If the answer is no, the facilitator calls for and records reasons for affirming the mission statement as it stands.
- If the answer is yes, the facilitator calls for and records suggestions for changing the mission.

If the mission is to be changed, the facilitator notes that the Assessment Team is responsible for developing a new mission statement, which the board chairman will present to the full board for approval.

XIII.	40 min.	Recommend goals.

The facilitator briefly reviews the definitions of goals, then gives participants ten minutes to either take time alone or discuss with others their thoughts on the organization's future direction and to write down three to five overarching goals. The facilitator then records suggestions on a flip chart and leads a large-group discussion to gain agreement on three to five roughly worded goals. The facilitator notes that the Assessment Team will confirm goals for the plan, and the board chairman will present them to the full board for approval.

XIV. 5 min. Review the next steps.

A member of the Assessment Team briefly reviews next steps in the self-assessment process: The Assessment Team will develop a new mission statement (if needed), confirm goals and results, and coordinate development of the plan and its presentation to the board for approval.

XV. 10 min. Conduct the closing.

The facilitator leads a reflective evaluation of the day's work and what participants are discovering about the organization through self-assessment. The board chairman or chief executive thanks all those who helped prepare the retreat, thanks participants, and closes the meeting.

Communicate purpose

The first factor in successful discussions is clarity of purpose. The overriding purpose of self-assessment group discussions or a retreat is to build common knowledge and commitment to the organization's mission, goals, and results. This happens through an exchange of thought and opinion in which constructive dissent is encouraged. There is a specific set of objectives for each session. Participants should receive advance agendas and have the opportunity to be well prepared by reviewing summary reports, completing readings and worksheets in the Participant Workbook, and (if they can be provided) by attending orientation sessions.

Clarify decision making

The combined insight of all participants forms the basis for decisions in the self-assessment process. It is up to the writer and Assessment Team to synthesize participants' input and shape it into reports and a draft plan. In the majority of cases, group recommendations and conclusions are sound and easily captured. However, when the Assessment Team has a significant question or concern, the team may go back to participants for more input or, as appropriate, make the critical judgment.

It is important that decision-making authority be clear to all self-assessment participants at the start.

- The board chairman has responsibility for the final review of the mission, goals, and budget, which are presented to the full board for approval.
- The chief executive, with the management team, is responsible for developing objectives, action steps, and a detailed budget. (The objectives are presented to the board for information.)

Encourage contribution

The ideal group discussion is one in which all participants contribute, and each person's comments are listened to and considered with equal attention. Establishing ground rules at the beginning of the first session helps encourage constructive dissent and define how discussion can be most productive. A more detailed discussion on encouraging contribution is included in Resource 3 (Effective Facilitation).

Members of the Assessment Team—and especially the board chairman and chief executive—should be very aware of how their participation affects the group. It is important that their thoughts be known, but at the same time they must be cautious not to dominate discussion or inhibit the contributions of others. Depth interviews offer an additional opportunity for individuals in leadership positions to be heard.

Summary report

When following Design Option A, Step 2 concludes with a report of participants' conclusions in the first group discussion. When following Design Option B, move to Step 5, Prepare and Distribute Final Report. The summary report presents agreement on the following:

A. The organization's most significant challenges
B. The organization's most significant opportunities
C. The primary customer
D. How primary customers will change
E. What we believe primary customers value
F. Supporting customers and what we believe they value
G. How supporting customers will change

H. New customers; customers to stop serving

I. Knowledge we want to gain from our customers

J. Whether the mission needs to be revisited

A sample summary report follows, in Exhibit 5.

Exhibit 5

Sample Summary of First Group Discussion

The first self-assessment group discussions were held separately with board and staff in November. Fourteen board members and all staff were present. The meetings were tape-recorded, and the following combined summary reflects input from flip chart notes, participant notes that were handed in, and recorded comments.

A. Most significant challenges:
- Decline of federal funds; fast-moving changes in state and county funding
- Overdependence on government funding
- Bound to "eligible participants" as defined by government
  - Influences not only *who* we serve but what services we can provide and over what length of time
- How to obtain funds, develop relationships, and enhance staff skills to meet needs of current and prospective participants
- Number and diversity of important partnerships and collaborations and significant time these require
- Changing demographics of area; increased diversity not reflected within staff or board of agency
- Increasingly complex needs of participants that go well beyond what can be addressed by traditional employment services
- Marketing ourselves; we are not known beyond narrow circles, do not have a strong community presence

B. Most significant opportunities:
- Potential to influence and play a significant role in area school-to-work curricula development and service design
  - Potential for new funds from local sources
- Potential to influence and play a significant role in area welfare-to-work philosophies, service design, and funding patterns
- Potential to have a broader impact on ability of service area residents to find and keep employment and advance to better-paying jobs
  - Funding sources may support service to those not currently eligible: Career assessment, counseling, and job placement services on a fee-for-service basis
- Ability to influence state and county employment service policies and funding decisions (already on "right" committees, attending forums, visiting elected officials)
- Potential to provide greater value to area employers
  - Help filling positions
  - Training needs
  - Ongoing human resources support
  - Potential to gain fee-based work

- Potential to be more broadly understood and supported as a community resource
- Potential to provide leadership in development of coordinated systems in area to ensure integrated support for *all* employment-related needs of participants

C. Primary customer

The following were suggested:

- Dislocated workers
- Non-English-speaking people
- Welfare recipients/AFDC recipients
- At-risk youth
- Disadvantaged youth and adults
- Older workers
- Unemployed people
- Underemployed people
- Low-income, single heads of households

Both groups agreed on the following definition of primary customers: *people who are unemployed, underemployed, or at risk for unemployment.*

It was also agreed that employers are *supporting* customers, but very important ones.

D. How primary customers will change:

- More customers who are welfare recipients
- More non-English-speaking customers
- More dislocated workers
- More single-parent families
- More older workers
- More people with disabilities
- More participants with multiple barriers to employment:
  Few skills
  Family dysfunction, violence
  Legal problems
  Chemical dependency
  Emotional problems
- More "hard core" youth; gang members

E. What we believe primary customers value:

- Welfare recipients/AFDC recipients
  Child care
  Transportation
  Tuition assistance
  Marketable skills

Exhibit 5 (continued)

Being treated with respect
Being able to control their own lives
Feeling more safe and secure
Opportunity to succeed (being off welfare)
Support mechanisms (monetary, personal)
Guidance, listening ear
Network of services, referrals

- At-risk youth
    Money or economic benefit
    Peer friendships/socializing
    Independence
    Opportunity for employment
    Feeling worthwhile
    Hope, another chance
- General unemployed or underemployed/dislocated workers
    Support/reassurance
    Training/retraining
    Being self-supporting
    Opportunity to start over
    Maintain current lifestyle
    Immediate reemployment at livable wage
    Someone to listen, encouragement
    Supplemental employment (beyond Social Security, pensions)
    Options/choices
    Information

F. Supporting customers and what we believe they value

- Employers:
    Quality/trained workforce
    Customized training resource
- County boards:
    Efficient use of resources
    More taxpayers; lower taxes
    Positive public relations
- Federal and state government:
    Meeting performance standards
    Success stories
    Cost-effectiveness; return on investment
- Educational systems/institutions:
    Services for at-risk youth
    Shared staff
    Educational materials

- Training institutions:
    - Students
    - Funding
- Private grantors:
    - Fiscal accountability
    - Quantifiable results
- Social service organizations:
    - Assessment of client needs
    - Smooth interaction
    - Collaboration on new funding opportunities
- Media:
    - Accountability
    - Good stories
    - Readers
- Business associations:
    - Reliable partner
    - Direction and support
    - Good labor pool
    - Job subsidies
    - Good public relations
    - Reliable information
- Staff:
    - Direction and support
    - Professional development
    - Resources to "do the job"
    - Seeing results
- Taxpayers:
    - Good use of public funds
    - That our primary customers are employed and contribute to society
- Primary customers (as word-of-mouth referral sources):
    - Good service, have needs met
    - Jobs/education/training
- Parents:
    - Paycheck for teenager
    - Direction and support for their kids

G. How supporting customers will change

- Government at all levels to seek lower numbers of people on welfare
- Private funders to seek innovative approaches to employment needs but will not sustain ongoing funding
- Small and mid-sized employers have more human resource "problems" like large employers, but do not have same access to staff and programs.

Exhibit 5 (continued)

- Employers to need higher-skilled workers
- Education and training institutions to need better links with employers
- Social service agencies and business associations to need reliable and flexible partners who know the employment field

H. New customers; customers to stop serving

- We should be serving youth beginning in middle school rather than near graduation. (Reason: clearer focus for youth on postgraduation direction, stronger employment skills.)
- People who are unemployed, underemployed, or at risk for unemployment who formerly did not qualify for STARS services because of federal eligibility guidelines should be considered new primary customers. We should be serving people as soon as *they* recognize their own need, as opposed to when their financial or employment situation has "fallen" to current eligibility levels. (Reason: fewer people reaching a crisis stage, more people able to *better* their situation, stronger workforce with necessary skills, stronger employers and stronger local economy.)
- We need to view private funders as "new" supporting customers—our approaches in the past have been extremely limited. (Reason: raise additional funds to support service to expanded population.)
- There are no customers we currently serve we should stop serving.

I. Knowledge we want to gain from our customers

Primary customers

- What do participants feel they need to change in their own life to get where they want to go?
- What are people's barriers to employment? Do they recognize them?
- What skills do people want to develop?
- What employment-related services do people want?
- What hours and locations do people want?
- How fast do people want service to be available once they contact us?
- How satisfied have customers been with STARS' services? What do they value most?

Supporting customers

- What challenges are employers facing from their own perspective that we might help address?
- What services do employers want and will they pay for them?
- Will private funders support expanded services?
- What STARS services are most valued by other community agencies?
- What additional roles do other community agencies think STARS should play?
- Do other community agencies see value in partnering with STARS?

J. Does the mission need to be revisited?

The general consensus was that the mission needs to be revisited.
Comments:

- Too restrictive on who we serve
- Should include employers
- Too long
- Should refer to partnering or collaboration
- Should match with our strategies
- Need clearer statement
- New mission should refocus our direction and allow expanded services

Follow-up

Immediately following group discussions or a retreat, the summary report is written, reviewed, and approved by the Assessment Team and distributed to all participants. In the case of a first group discussion, the Assessment Team meets to move forward on customer research and depth interviews. Following a retreat, see Step 5.

STEP 3 Conduct customer research and depth interviews

The voice of the customer

In the environmental scan, you went outside the organization to discover facts and trends likely to affect the organization in its future work. Most environmental scanning makes use of existing information, although you may have conducted interviews with select key informants. At this point you focus on customers—with emphasis on the primary customer—and go directly to them to gain insight into what they value and how they view the organization. If you have existing information about the organization's customers, it may certainly be used and interpreted as part of self-assessment customer research. However, if the information is outdated, incomplete, or does not adequately answer the question What does the customer value? then new research with your current and future customers is essential.

The purpose of customer research is to bring the voice of the customer directly into the organization's discussions and decision making. Research produces firsthand information on customers' needs, wants, and aspirations—what they value.

Customer-research design

Your design for customer research is based on what and how much knowledge you need to gain. Potential research questions are drafted and handed in during the first group discussion or developed by the Assessment Team in advance of a retreat. (See Worksheet 8 in the Participant Workbook.) A customer-research task force or the Assessment Team, possibly with guidance from qualified volunteers or paid consultants, is responsible for refining questions and designing the overall research effort, including, to the greatest degree possible, roles for self-assessment participants. The chief executive is responsible for the research effort. Specific tasks may be assigned to staff, board members, volunteers, the facilitator, or others.

Deciding who should conduct and analyze customer research can be provocative. There are two schools of thought. The first is the "Objective Outsider" school, which holds that only people not directly associated with the organization can make customers feel truly comfortable enough to speak their mind and that only outsiders can ensure that research findings are valid and free of personal bias. The "Involved Insider" school argues for the importance of people associated with the organization hearing directly from customers about what they value; examples are given in which, with proper training, this has been a compelling experience that produces valid findings. In addition, a cost-effectiveness case can be made for this approach, as it reduces dependence on outside help. A happy medium is sometimes reached through the use of qualified volunteers.

The scope of the research effort also influences the design for carrying it out. Some large-scale projects reach hundreds of customers. Others contact a handful. Here are seven design examples:

1. A national membership organization took six months to:
   - Hire a research firm to conduct five hundred telephone interviews and produce a detailed analysis.
   - Use a paid professional to design and analyze responses from a questionnaire that one hundred local presidents used to interview each other during a national meeting.
   - Use a paid professional to train self-assessment participants as focus group facilitators and recorders who, in turn, ran fourteen focus groups simultaneously during a national conference. The professional then summarized findings.

Note: Customer research and depth interviews can be conducted simultaneously and, when following Design Option B, may take place as part of Phase One, Step 6.

- Use a paid professional to train an Assessment Team member who, in turn, prepared other self-assessment participants to conduct twenty face-to-face interviews with supporting customers; results were analyzed by the Assessment Team member.

2. A vocational rehabilitation agency took one month to do the following:
- Use self-assessment participants to analyze twenty-five past customers' program evaluations and staff follow-up notes.
- Design phone surveys and assign staff members to conduct and analyze interviews with fifteen primary customers and their rehabilitation counselors.

3. An art museum contracted with a market research firm and took three months to:
- Hold a videotaped series of focus groups with two proposed new customer groups that historically had not visited the museum in great numbers.
- Analyze results and produce a summary report.
- Edit highlights of the videotapes into a fifteen-minute segment as part of a special presentation of findings for self-assessment participants and, later, the board.

4. A local public health organization took six weeks to:
- Use staff to conduct and analyze a mail-back customer satisfaction survey.

5. A large United Way organization took five months to:
- Form a research task force with Assessment Team members and volunteer research professionals.
- Use a paid consultant to facilitate initial task force meetings and coach a staff member in developing interview and focus group formats using a blend of original questions and a standard United Way of America format.
- Use volunteer research professionals and student interns under the direction of a pro bono research firm to analyze responses from two hundred leadership donors and volunteers selected by the Assessment Team.
- Use self-assessment participants to debrief campaign volunteers on what they were learning in the course of calling on accounts.
- Develop an interview format with the assistance of a school superintendent, train United Way board members, and complete assignments for interviews with elementary school principals in board members' home school districts.

6. A county government assessing services for homeless people formed a partnership with a research foundation that helped the county:
- Design a face-to-face interview format.
- Recruit and train one hundred volunteers, including self-assessment participants.
- Use volunteers to conduct three hundred interviews with homeless people in shelters across the county in one night.
- Analyze results and produce a summary report.

7. A battered women's shelter took two weeks to:
   - Convene a focus group discussion with battered women's advocates, many of whom were former victims, to ask how the shelter could be more effective.
   - Plan and conduct a one-hour "telethon" during a regular evening meeting for all board members to call lists of donors to say "thank you" and ask what these donors value about the organization.

The design of each organization's research effort depends on individual circumstances and needs. Examples of customer-research formats are provided in Exhibit 6. Develop a design that produces the knowledge you need to gain from your customers, brings powerful statements of what customers value into the self-assessment process, and best employs the organization's human and financial resources.

To learn directly from customers what they value, the Assessment Team does the following:

- Determines what information is needed from customers.
- If needed, obtains volunteer or paid assistance to design customer research.
- Determines as specifically as possible the questions research will answer.
- Identifies information already available within the organization that helps answer research questions, including existing studies, statistics, reports, and the knowledge of staff and volunteers who interact with customers.
- Identifies customer groups for research and the number of individuals to be contacted.
- Decides whether and in what settings to conduct surveys, focus groups, individual interviews, or other forms of research; develops formats.
- Decides who will conduct and analyze the research and how self-assessment participants will be involved.
- Sets a research budget if paid consultants are to be involved.
- Determines whether training will be needed for nonprofessional researchers.
- Develops a work plan for the research effort and a deadline for its completion.

Exhibit 6

Sample Customer-Research Formats for STARS, Inc.

Questions for Customer Research

The following questions were generated by board and staff in first group discussions.

Primary customers

- What do participants feel they need to change in their own life to get where they want to go?
- What are people's barriers to employment? Do they recognize them?
- What skills do people want to develop?
- What employment-related services do people want?
- What hours and locations do people want?
- How fast do people want service to be available once they contact us?
- How satisfied have customers been with STARS' services? What do they value most?

Supporting customers

- What challenges are employers facing from their own perspective that we might help address?
- What services do employers want, and will they pay for them?
- Will private funders support expanded services?
- What STARS services are most valued by other community agencies?
- What additional roles do other community agencies think STARS should play?
- Do other community agencies see value in partnering with STARS?

Customer-Research Design

1. Reach thirty primary customers—present or past—through focus groups in three locations. Surveys to be completed in groups. If thirty cannot attend groups, reach additional participants for phone interviews.

   - Facilitator to assist with question path
   - Deputy director to develop list of services for survey
   - Staff planner to conduct focus groups and interviews

2. Reach fifteen employers through focus groups "tacked on" to Chamber of Commerce meeting and Regional Economic Development Council meeting. Surveys to be completed in groups.

   - Facilitator to assist with question path
   - Board members to help with list of potential services to employers for survey
   - Board members to help arrange with chamber and council staff
   - Staff planner to conduct focus groups

Exhibit 6 (continued)

3. Reach twenty who are representative of community agencies and educational institutions through specially convened focus groups. Surveys to be completed in groups.

   • Facilitator to assist with question path
   • Primary customer list of services available
   • Executive director to send letter of invitation; administrative assistant will handle RSVPs
   • Staff planner to conduct focus groups

4. Analyze published information on private funders for fit with STARS mission and possible future directions.

   • Executive director to handle

Primary Customer Focus Group and Phone Interview Question Path

1. What have you liked best about your experiences with STARS?
2. What have you liked least about your experiences with STARS?
3. What do we do for you that you really value? What really helps you?
4. Are there gaps in the services we provide?
5. Are there services we offer that we could or should eliminate?
6. How could we expand or supplement our services to better meet your needs?
7. If you could custom design our services, what would they be like?

Supporting Customer Focus Group Question Path (Employers)

1. If someone asked you to tell them about STARS, what would you say?
2. As an employer, what challenges are you facing in terms of recruiting and retaining employees?
3. What are the biggest changes you have experienced in the labor market over the past five years?
4. What changes do you see ahead?
5. What sort of needs do you have for employee training beyond what your business already provides?
6. Based on your knowledge of STARS, what should we do differently?

Supporting Customer Focus Group Question Path (Community Agencies and Educational Institutions)

1. If someone asked you to tell them about STARS, what would you say?
2. What are the greatest barriers facing your customers or clientele today regarding their readiness or access to employment and training programs?

3. What does STARS do for your customers that they really value? What really helps them?
4. How do you view STARS' services in relationship to what you do? How does what we do complement the services your organization provides?
5. Are there gaps in the services we provide? What are they?
6. How could STARS expand or supplement our services to better meet the needs of your customers? Are there things we should be doing that we are not?
7. Are there services that STARS should cut back or eliminate?
8. If you could custom design our services, what would they be like?

Exhibit 6 (continued)

Primary Customer Survey

Following is a list of STARS services. Please rank them according to their importance to you.

Service	Couldn't live without	Very important	Somewhat important	Not important
Vocational/Career counseling	☐	☐	☐	☐
Aptitude/Interest assessment	☐	☐	☐	☐
STEPS workshop	☐	☐	☐	☐
Employment planning	☐	☐	☐	☐
Life skills training (self-esteem, goal setting, personal financial management, and so forth)	☐	☐	☐	☐
Financial help with schooling	☐	☐	☐	☐
Customized training	☐	☐	☐	☐
On-the-job training	☐	☐	☐	☐
Literacy services, including translation for non-English speaking, English as second language, help with GED, and so forth	☐	☐	☐	☐
Information on how to look for a job	☐	☐	☐	☐
Workshops teaching "world of work" skills (what employers want)	☐	☐	☐	☐
How to start your own business training	☐	☐	☐	☐
Local labor market information	☐	☐	☐	☐
Help in applying for and starting work	☐	☐	☐	☐
Help for problems during training	☐	☐	☐	☐
Help for problems after starting work	☐	☐	☐	☐
Support services (child care, transportation, help with crises)	☐	☐	☐	☐
Motivation, support, encouragement	☐	☐	☐	☐

I would recommend STARS' services to others: ☐ Yes ☐ No

Other services that may be helpful (please specify):

Supporting Customer Survey (Employers)

Please rank the following services based on their importance to you as an employer.

Service	Couldn't live without	Very important	Somewhat important	Not important	Would consider contracting for this
Assessment of potential employees (skill, aptitude, interest, work values)	☐	☐	☐	☐	☐ Yes
Customized training (specifically developed for your business)	☐	☐	☐	☐	☐ Yes
On-the-job training (for one or more employees for a specific job)	☐	☐	☐	☐	☐ Yes
Job readiness training (preparing a potential employee for the work world—being on time, accepting supervision, conflict resolution, and so forth)	☐	☐	☐	☐	☐ Yes
New employee follow-up services (problem solving, conflict resolution, help with transportation, and so forth)	☐	☐	☐	☐	☐ Yes
In-house employee seminars (time management, effective communication, supervisory skills training, and so forth)	☐	☐	☐	☐	☐ Yes
Listing positions, recruitment, screening	☐	☐	☐	☐	☐ Yes
Job analysis (in-depth job descriptions along with necessary skills for effective performance)	☐	☐	☐	☐	☐ Yes
Labor market information	☐	☐	☐	☐	☐ Yes
Employer information (Americans with Disabilities Act, Workers Compensation, and so forth)	☐	☐	☐	☐	☐ Yes
Literacy services including translation for non-English speakers, referrals to English as a Second Language class, and so forth	☐	☐	☐	☐	☐ Yes

Exhibit 6 (continued)

Service	Couldn't live without	Very important	Somewhat important	Not important	Would consider contracting for this
Human resource assistance (problem situations with employees, sexual harassment, potential terminations, chemical dependency issues, and so forth)	☐	☐	☐	☐	☐ Yes

Supporting Customer Survey (Community Agencies and Educational Institutions)

Following is a list of STARS services. Please rank them according to their importance to your customers or clientele.

Service	Couldn't live without	Very important	Somewhat important	Not important
Vocational/Career counseling	☐	☐	☐	☐
Aptitude/Interest assessment	☐	☐	☐	☐
STEPS workshop	☐	☐	☐	☐
Employment planning	☐	☐	☐	☐
Life skills training (self-esteem, goal setting, personal financial management, and so forth)	☐	☐	☐	☐
Financial help with schooling	☐	☐	☐	☐
Customized training	☐	☐	☐	☐
On-the-job training	☐	☐	☐	☐
Literacy services, including translation for non-English speaking, English as second language, help with GED, and so forth	☐	☐	☐	☐
Information on how to look for a job	☐	☐	☐	☐
Workshops teaching "world of work" skills (what employers want)	☐	☐	☐	☐
How to start your own business training	☐	☐	☐	☐
Local labor market information	☐	☐	☐	☐
Help in applying for and starting work	☐	☐	☐	☐
Help for problems during training	☐	☐	☐	☐
Help for problems after starting work	☐	☐	☐	☐
Support services (child care, transportation, help with crises)	☐	☐	☐	☐
Motivation, support, encouragement	☐	☐	☐	☐

We would consider contracting for one or more of these services: ☐ Yes   ☐ No

Other services that may be helpful (please specify):

▨ Report of customer-research findings

Those responsible for analyzing research collaborate with the writer to develop the draft customer-research report. The report states key findings with each customer group and may support general findings with numerical analyses or highlights of individual responses. The report cites sources and may include appendixes with descriptions of research participants and research techniques. Copies of full customer responses may also be prepared for self-assessment participants who request them.

A sample customer report follows (Exhibit 7).

Exhibit 7

Sample Customer-Research Report for STARS, Inc.

Customer-research efforts were led by the STARS staff planner with assistance from other staff in setting up and conducting primary customer focus groups and surveys. Board members assisted in recruiting employers to participate in focus groups. The facilitator assisted with customer-research design.

> Twenty-eight primary customers participated in focus groups or responded to surveys
> Fourteen employers participated in focus groups
> Thirty-five representatives of community agencies participated in focus groups

A. Findings with Primary Customers

General findings

Participants are satisfied with STARS' services overall and particularly appreciate the professional, personable, and supportive work of staff. Customers said greater value could be provided through the following:

- Help with issues related to employment, specifically, low-cost housing, personal financial management, day care and transportation assistance, more financial assistance training, and periods of transition
- Extend schooling opportunities to more than one year
- More job variety; more upper-level openings from employers
- More help preparing for job interviews and understanding what employers are looking for
- More individualized service with one primary counselor for all needs
- Better explanation of all services available; no jargon
- Providing support groups or mentors
- All counselors visiting on campus vs. coming to your office
- Office hours and programs in the evening
- No waiting time for service to begin
- Doing follow-up interest testing over time
- Improving or removing one of STARS' partner agencies that helps with job placement once STARS has completed assessments. It does not appear to be operating effectively, giving rise to frustrations
- STARS should be better known; easier to find out about

Selected comments

> "Not everyone is being given the same information."
> "Your job placement agency is not as good as you are."

Exhibit 7 (continued)

"Do everything that is currently being done. Push the state for more funds so that you can provide more services."

"They treat you as a person, not just another case."

"Without the financial aid I could *not* have attended school."

"It was hard to talk with my staff person when it fit my schedule."

"Offer more motivational workshops."

"Gave me hope, changed my life."

"Get the word out better."

Top-rated services

Ranked by most "couldn't live without" and "very important" ratings:

1. Financial help with schooling
2. Support services (child care, transportation, and so forth)
3. Motivation, support, encouragement
4. Aptitude, interest assessment
5. Life skills training (self-esteem, goal setting, personal financial management)
6. On-the-job training
7. Local labor market information
8. Vocational and career counseling

B. Findings with Supporting Customers (Employers)

General findings

Employers' greatest challenge is getting and keeping qualified employees. This is partly seen as a matter of a "lower-skilled" labor pool with "questionable work ethics" and partly a matter of scarcity of time and resources for initial and ongoing training and support. Employers see increasing competition for good workers, a lack of low-cost housing and transportation, a need for higher technical skills, and an aging and diversifying workforce.

Selected comments from employers on how they see STARS

- "An organization available to provide consultative assistance to employers."
- "Helps place potential employees with employers. Helps people find jobs that are subsidized with government dollars."
- "One-stop shop where people can seek help for education and job placement."
- "You need to market yourselves."

Top-rated services

Ranked by most "couldn't live without" and "very important" ratings, as well as willingness to contract out for such services:

1. Employer information seminars (Americans with Disabilities Act, Workers' Compensation, and so forth)
2. Human resource assistance (problem situations, sexual harassment, potential terminations, chemical dependency issues, and so forth)
3. Literacy services, including translators, English as a Second Language classes
4. Assessment of potential employees
5. Basic employment skills training
6. Recruiting and screening applicants
7. Job analysis (determining skills necessary for effective performance)

C. Findings with Supporting Customers (Community Agencies and Educational Institutions)

General findings

Agencies view STARS positively as "a place where a person can get help with job training, job experience, interest testing, job placement, and overcoming employment barriers." STARS is seen as building collaborative relationships and is noted for "bringing funding to the table." There were no suggestions for eliminating any STARS services. Recommendations for expanding STARS activity include:

- Start the process earlier with youth; focus on those who "can and will raise hell."
- Hold workshops, counseling sessions in schools and on campus; be part of new student orientations; be more integrated in education systems.
- Expand hours and be more flexible in scheduling appointments; quicker "turn-around."
- Expand networking with business.
- Help expand availability of child care.
- Be a key player in welfare reform.
- Focus more on job-readiness skills, employment preparation.
- Be more "mission focused" instead of "driven by government funding"; develop local resources.
- Communicate better what STARS is and what it can do.
- Expand scope to include a broader base of people.
- Play an earlier and more central coordinating role as "jobs case manager."
- Help teach work ethic.
- Expand current services, operate on a larger scale.

Exhibit 7 (continued)

Top-rated services

Ranked by most "couldn't live without" and "very important" ratings in terms of importance to community agencies' customers:

1. Support services (child care, transportation, and so forth)
2. Financial help with schooling
3. Workshops teaching "world of work" skills; job readiness training
4. Life skills training (self-esteem, goal setting, personal financial management, and so forth)
5. Aptitude/Interest assessment
6. Help in applying for and starting work; help for problems that come up
7. On-the-job training
8. Motivation, support, encouragement

Agencies responded they *would* consider contracting out for the top-rated services.

D. Findings with Supporting Customers (Private Funders)

General findings

Staff reviewed profiles of foundations that cover the Southwest area and have an employment-related focus. Six foundations were identified as a strong fit, with two specifically interested in welfare-to-work initiatives. The executive director attended an informational meeting where both of these funders made presentations and feels there are strong immediate funding opportunities based on the direction of self-assessment discussions to date.

An informal discussion on the topic of seeking contributed funds directly from area employers was held at a board meeting. Employers on the board felt STARS would need to establish a much higher profile in the community and do a better job of proving its overall value to the area economy before employers would be receptive to direct contributions. However, board members also emphasized STARS' opportunity to develop and provide contracted services to employers, as there is both "a need and a gap in the market in this area."

◼ Depth interviews

Depth interviews enrich the self-assessment process by highlighting the insights of a select group of individuals inside the organization. These findings preview the topics of the retreat or second group discussion and provide a touchstone for group discussion and decision making.

The Assessment Team designs depth interviews, possibly with guidance from the facilitator or a consultant. Interviews are generally conducted and summarized by the facilitator. They can take place in person, by telephone, or, at the request of depth interview participants, as a set of written responses.

Those invited to participate in depth interviews may be board members, staff, or key volunteers and usually include the board chairman and chief executive, who are responsible for securing agreements to participate in depth interviews. Six to twelve depth interviews are usually conducted with a cross-section of participants who:

- Have views considered to be specially valuable.
- May choose to hold back in group discussions so as not to be perceived as dominating the process.
- Are known to be vocal, opinionated, and a better group participant if given an advance opportunity to contribute.
- Require extra attention.
- Are known to give their best in one-to-one discussion rather than in a group.
- Are nonconformists whose views may not otherwise get a fair hearing in group discussion.
- Were asked to participate in a retreat or group discussions but are unable to attend.

Here is a set of basic depth interview questions. If pointed issues have already arisen through the self-assessment process, additional questions, like the samples following, may be asked:

1. What is your role with [the organization] and what is the length of your involvement?
2. The current mission of the organization is to. . . . Do you believe the mission should be revisited? Why or why not?
3. What do you see as the most significant challenges to the organization in the coming years?
4. What are the most significant opportunities?
5. Is the organization successful? Why or why not?
6. What should be the organization's results in changed lives?

7. What programs should be strengthened, considered for abandonment, or analyzed?
8. Are there internal systems that should be assessed for potential improvement?
9. Should the mission be changed?
   If the present mission should be affirmed, why is that?
   If the mission should be revised, what do you recommend?
10. Are there true innovations the organization should consider?
11. If it were up to you to set the organization's overarching goals for the future, what would they be?
12. Is there any other aspect of self-assessment you would like to comment on?

Sample "pointed issue" questions are:

- Do you favor the idea of launching a $50-million endowment drive next year? Why or why not?
- With the information available at this time, do you favor the proposed merger?
- What questions about the merger still need to be answered?
- There has been quite a bit of discussion about taking a more public advocacy stance on social policies. Do you believe the organization should change its advocacy role? Why or why not?

To design depth interviews, the Assessment Team does the following:

1. Confirms depth interview participants
2. Determines questions
3. Decides who will conduct and summarize interviews
4. Sets a deadline for their completion

When depth interviews are completed, the interviewer is responsible for developing a preliminary summary for review by the Assessment Team. A sample depth interview report follows in Exhibit 8.

Exhibit 8

Sample Depth Interview Report for STARS, Inc.

1. Participant profile

Depth interviews were conducted by the facilitator with the board chairman, six other board members, the executive director, and the deputy director. The nine individuals interviewed represent a cumulative total of eighty-two years experience with STARS.

2. Should the mission be revisited? Why or why not?

Yes: 8
- Too restrictive
- Statement too long, too cumbersome

No: 1
- Don't need to change: Looks good, is what we are

3. What are the most significant challenges?

- Changes involving government policy:
  Employers having to contribute and/or pay for service
  Population base in service delivery area below 200,000, affecting formula dollars
  Welfare reform putting more pressure on counties
  Future state role, ongoing relationship with elected and agency officials
- Adequate funding
- More collaboration
  Structures to work together that go beyond differing rules and regulations that separate and promote single-focus agencies
  Greater networking capability
- Where and how do we move forward other than in traditional areas in which we've been involved?
- Harder and harder to serve people; complex, difficult situations
- Public awareness of what we're all about

4. What are the most significant opportunities?

- Opening up new avenues for training:
  Getting to industries and businesses as customers; how to serve them?

Exhibit 8 (continued)

- Exploring new avenues for programming and service:
  Offering fee-based services
- Expanding our network with counties, school districts, other networking agencies
- Contracting with other counties, agencies:
  Providing cost-effective services
- More programs on more cost-effective basis for all kids
  Our diverse population opening us up to do new and different things
- Networking with business and industry
- Public awareness of what we're all about

5. Is the organization successful? Why or why not?

Based on the organization's current mission and definition of results, all felt STARS is successful. However, they noted that customers identified a number of areas for improvement.

Successful because:

- Good staff:
  Executive director/administration strong and well respected
- Dedicated, flexible
- Have customers' best interests at heart, sincerely want people to succeed
- Good performance results: highly respected on state and national levels
- Strong board, involved in local communities across fourteen-county area
- Honesty shown in financial audit; being clean, on top of things
- Keeping up on county, local changes that affect us
- Well-established networks, ties, especially with family service and educational institutions
- Good internal communications
- Stretching the dollar; region allows more opportunities to do so

Not successful because organization:

- Lacks vision, future planning:
  Is stagnant, as opposed to looking in new directions to expand; lack of future vision
  Needs more open staff, aggressive in pursuit of opportunities rather than accepting of what comes along
  Needs executive director to have and convey a vision for the future
  Shouldn't settle into routine and not look beyond
  Can't get "out of the box" at executive board level
- Lacks political muscle:
  Needs plan for "getting on the inside"

- Doesn't go far enough in helping customers to "change lives"; stops at three-month follow-up after a first job and often can't offer additional service that would be helpful.
- Board composition does not adequately reflect best "influence leader" composition across sectors.
- Needs more effective board in making valuable connections and representing mission to area communities.
- Hasn't paid enough attention to business and employers as customers.
- Lacks recognition by general public.
- Shows hesitancy verging on inability to take risks.
- Has limited dollars that are restricted to certain populations.
- Has dwindling source of money in past few years.
- Decides what to do on the basis of state mandates rather than what best serves people in our service area.
- Needs board members more directly involved in pubic relations.
- Needs to do a better job at being at cutting edge.
  Needs a budget reserve for new initiatives, risk taking

6. *What should the organization's results be?*

- Numbers, government performance indicators: high placement rates at good wages
- Good training that makes a difference in important skills
- Help to people so they have lifelong ability to develop their career
- A qualified workforce
- Movement of people from welfare dependency to self-sufficiency
- Movement of people from school to work
- Basic hope for people who need training or retraining to get into the mainstream
- A better-trained workforce—more confident, self-reliant, and positive-thinking
- Customer satisfaction reports: What customers say about how their lives have been improved; often quite meaningful and emotional

Comments:
- Help more people, be more recognized, and have more ways to measure the extent of our impact.
- More follow-up to know how long people remain employed, if they move up in an organization, in their career, and so forth.
- Continue and enhance performance against indicators.
- Expand results to broader-based population, take it out to everyone.
- Provide investment into our communities. Bring people, monetary investment into local economies

Exhibit 8 (continued)

7. *What programs should be strengthened, abandoned, or analyzed?*

Strengthen

- Continue to work with government-funded programs and make necessary changes; for example, make transitions with welfare reform:
  Expand our county relationships.
- Form closer alliances with postsecondary education.
- Forge broader and deeper business and industry partnerships.
- Work collaboratively with other agencies to meet clients' needs.
  Expand our services to the population in general.

Abandon

- We have limited our scope, have very strong core services, nothing to abandon.
- Little to abandon; need to expand.
- Need to fix or abandon the relationship with current placement group, even if it's politically incorrect: Customers are frustrated, and so is staff.

Analyze

- Lessen dependence on government; set and meet goals for percentage of budget to be nongovernment funds.

8. *Are there internal systems that should be assessed for potential improvement?*

- Need to dedicate a very strong staff person to financial resource development; grants, contracts, other funds.
- Address political, social, and economic factors that will be affecting us:
  Ensure ongoing good political connections.
- Increase breadth and depth of overall board involvement:
  Bring committed new members to board, especially executive committee.
  Open up more decision making beyond executive board.
  Get better information before meetings.
- Set aside dollars for new initiatives.
- Raise our profile, build image, get much more recognition:
  As *the* employment and training resource for individuals and agencies.
- Need to unleash our highly qualified staff to be flexible to meet the needs of clients, whether employers or employees:
  Encourage entrepreneurial spirit and give meaningful rewards and recognition for this.

9. Should the mission be revised?

Yes: 8
- Should be less restrictive on eligibility.
- Statement is too long, too cumbersome.
- Bottom line: Help people get jobs and have the ability to develop a career long term.

No: 1

10. Are there true innovations the organization should consider?

- Be proactive in school-to-work collaborations; be part of how education has to change to "move beyond the four walls":
  School staffs need to be trained to help students in school-based activities that relate to work.
  Internships and mentorships should be coordinated; provide support and documentation in employment settings to ensure work experience meets requirements for graduation rules.
  Take more leadership; be a direct avenue for the funding effort.
- Establish a fee-for-service department:
  Expand and market services to the community in general.
- Define and pursue a role in economic development:
  Our role in this is human resource development.

11. What are the overarching goals for the future?

- Continue to be a leader of employment and training in our area and expand to all primary customers with need.
- Lead in welfare-to-work and in school-to-work initiatives.
- Be a valued resource for area employers.
- Contribute to overall economic development of region.
- Develop ourselves financially.
- Develop a stronger board and better marketing capacities.

12. Is there any other aspect of self-assessment you would like to comment on?

- Favorable responses on the process to this point were given.

▦ Prepare and distribute reports

To complete this step, the Assessment Team does the following:

- Meets to review preliminary reports. Those who analyzed customer research and conducted depth interviews join the Assessment Team for this meeting.
- Makes editorial recommendations for final drafts.
- Gains approval of final drafts from the board chairman and chief executive.
- Decides whether to hold a customer-research and depth interview briefing prior to a second group discussion.
- Prepares a presentation for orientation sessions, briefings, the second group discussion, or retreat. One or more individuals are assigned to develop and present an overview of findings and respond to questions.
- Distributes customer-research and depth interview reports to self-assessment participants.

As with other reports, the customer-research and depth interview reports can be used to inform people in the organization who are not actively participating in the self-assessment process.

STEP 4 Hold group discussion on the fourth and fifth Drucker questions

Exhibit 9 provides objectives and an agenda for a second group discussion.

An introduction to successful group discussions or a retreat is provided in Step 2. A more detailed discussion of effective facilitation is in Resource 3.

Exhibit 9

Sample Agenda for a Second Group Discussion

Option A—Second Group Discussion

Sample Objectives and Agenda

Objectives

1. Revisit the mission and, if needed, propose change.
2. Outline what results for the organization should be.
3. Identify what must be strengthened, abandoned, or analyzed.
4. Recommend goals for the plan.

Agenda

    I. Extend welcome; give overview; review ground rules.
   II. Review customer-research and depth interview findings.
  III. Confirm what primary and supporting customers value.
  IV. Ask the question, Have we been successful? (Worksheets 10 and 11).
   V. Outline results (Worksheet 12).
  VI. Refreshment break
 VII. Identify what must be strengthened, abandoned, or analyzed (Worksheet 13).
VIII. Revisit the mission (Worksheets 4 and 14).
  IX. Recommend goals (Worksheet 15).
   X. Review next steps.
  XI. Conduct closing.

Total session time: 4 hours

Second Group Discussion: Sample Annotated Agenda

I.   5 min.   Extend welcome, give overview, review ground rules.

One or more members of the Assessment Team handles:
- General welcome
- Participant introductions (if needed)
- Discussion of purpose of the session, agenda overview, use of customer-research and depth interview findings
- Review of ground rules (facilitator)

II.   20 min.   Review customer-research and depth interview findings.

Customer-research and depth interview findings are presented by one or more members of the Assessment Team, followed by a question-and-answer period.

Exhibit 9 (continued)

III.   15 min.   Confirm what primary and supporting customers value.

In a large-group discussion, the facilitator seeks agreement on what primary customers value, then directs participants to review Worksheet 7 in light of this agreement and discuss differences from prior beliefs.

20 min.   Confirm what supporting customers value.

The facilitator divides participants into small groups, assigns each group one or more supporting customers, and gives ten minutes to confirm what the assigned customers value. Brief verbal reports are given in the large group, and what has been recorded in the small groups is collected for use by the writer.

IV.   15 min.   Discussion: Have we been successful?

The facilitator directs participants to Worksheets 10 and 11 and gives a few moments to discuss responses informally in pairs or small groups. The facilitator leads a large-group discussion to confirm the organization's current definition of results, then gains the group's response to the question, Have we been successful? and highlights the degrees of success with various customers.

V.   40 min.   Outline results.

At this point in the discussion, a change of pace is in order. Here is a suggested exercise: The facilitator reminds participants that the organization's results are in changed lives, then asks that everyone have paper and pen ready. The facilitator leads a short guided imagery in which participants are asked to imagine the organization has been chosen to receive a Presidential Citation for Excellence, which will be announced during the State of the Union Address. Seated as special guests in the Congressional Gallery, participants hear the president say, "I wish to cite [your organization] as an example to the nation in changing lives. I am certainly inspired by the overall performance of [your organization]. Let me share how lives have been changed. . . ." At this point, the facilitator tells participants they have two minutes to complete the president's thoughts and asks them to immediately begin writing.

The facilitator asks each participant in turn to contribute one result they thought of and records responses on a flip chart until all potential results have been suggested.

The facilitator completes this portion by asking for the group's judgment of what results should be. What is realistic, yet ambitious? What are the best results that people really believe could be achieved?

VI.   10 min.   Refreshment break

VII.   35 min.   Identify what must be strengthened, abandoned, or analyzed.

The facilitator places participants into four or five small groups and asks that they be mindful of discussion to this point as they complete their next assignment.

Groups are directed to Worksheet 13 and given fifteen minutes to agree on "candidates" for strengthening, abandonment, or analysis, as well as internal systems that should be assessed. Groups write their candidates on a piece of flip chart paper and post it. The large group is then given ten minutes to make a tour of the flip charts and write check marks next to the posted candidates with which they agree. The facilitator concludes this portion with discussion to confirm the group's priorities for potential strengthening, abandonment, analysis, and further assessment.

| VIII. | 30 min. | Ask whether the mission should be changed. |

The facilitator directs participants to Worksheet 14 and gives a moment for participants to review their response. The facilitator tells participants they are free to modify their original response, then asks for a show of hands on whether the mission should be changed. The facilitator asks for a group conclusion.

- If the answer is no, the facilitator calls for and records reasons for affirming the mission statement as it stands.
- If the answer is yes, the facilitator calls for and records suggestions for changing the mission.

If the mission is to be changed, the facilitator notes that the Assessment Team is responsible for developing a new mission statement, which the board chairman will present to the full board for approval.

| IX. | 35 min. | Recommend goals. |

The facilitator briefly reviews the definitions of goals, then gives participants ten minutes to either take time alone or discuss with others their thoughts on the organization's future direction and to write down three to five overarching goals. The facilitator then records suggestions on a flip chart and leads a large-group discussion to gain agreement on three to five roughly worded goals. The facilitator notes that the Assessment Team will confirm goals for the plan, and the board chairman will present them to the full board for approval.

| X. | 5 min. | Review next steps. |

A member of the Assessment Team briefly reviews next steps in the self-assessment process: The Assessment Team will develop a new mission statement (if needed), confirm goals and results, and coordinate development of the plan and its presentation to the board for approval.

| XI. | 10 min. | Conduct the closing. |

The facilitator leads a reflective evaluation of two group discussions and what participants are discovering about the organization through self-assessment. The board chairman or chief executive thanks all those who helped prepare the group discussion, thanks participants, and closes the meeting.

Phase Two concludes with a final report of participants' conclusions to this point in the self-assessment process. The report summarizes agreement on:

A. Whether the mission should be revised and, if so, what changes are proposed.

B. The organization's most significant challenges and opportunities

C. The primary customer

D. What primary customers value

E. Supporting customers

F. What supporting customers value

G. Whether the organization is successful and in what ways

H. What results should be

I. Programs that should be strengthened, abandoned, or analyzed

J. Internal systems that should be assessed

K. Draft

The writer, with guidance from the Assessment Team, is responsible for development of the final report (see Exhibit 10). The facilitator and others may be asked to assist. A polished draft of the report is distributed to the Assessment Team for review; the draft is edited and distributed.

Exhibit 10

Sample Final Report for STARS, Inc.

A. Whether the Mission Should Be Changed and, If So, Recommended Changes

The great majority of self-assessment participants said the mission should be changed. Suggestions include:

- Shorten and simplify
- Make it less restrictive so we can help all those in our communities who could benefit
- Include employers
- Include partnering and collaboration
- Bottom line: Help people get jobs and be able to develop careers so they are employable long term

B. Most Significant Challenges and Opportunities

Challenges

- Decreased federal funding; shift to state and county; need to diversify funding
- Increasing number of partnerships and collaborations
- Increasing numbers of "harder to serve" people
- Moving beyond current definition of "eligible participants"
- How to develop relationships and enhance staff skills to meet needs of current and prospective customers
- Changing demographics of area—increased diversity not reflected within staff or board of agency
- Raising community awareness of STARS, marketing its services and value

Opportunities

- Potential to influence and play a significant role in school-to-work initiatives
- Potential to play significant leadership role in welfare-to-work initiatives
- Potential to have a broader impact on ability of service area residents to find and keep employment and advance to better-paying jobs
- Opening up new avenues and methods for training
- Potential to provide greater value to area employers
- Potential to provide leadership in development of coordinated systems in area to ensure integrated support for *all* employment related needs of participants
- Potential to be more broadly understood and supported as a community resource

Exhibit 10 (continued)

C. The primary customer

People who are unemployed, underemployed, or at risk for unemployment

D. What primary customers value

- Personalized, caring service, ideally from one lead staff member
- An organization that instills self-esteem and hope; "people who know me and care about me"
- Funding for school or training and financial assistance with day care, transportation, and emergency needs
- A full range of employment information, services, and practical resources
- Employment-related workshops, job-seeking support groups
- Being treated professionally
- Immediate response when service is needed at convenient locations with flexible hours
- Clear information—enough but not too much
- The opportunity for follow-up and additional service over time

E. Supporting Customers

- Federal, state, and county funding agencies
- Employers
- Other community agencies
- Schools and training institutions
- Private funders
- Economic development organizations

F. What Supporting Customers Value

- Federal, state, and county funding agencies
  Accountability, meeting performance standards, fewer people on public assistance
- Employers
  Qualified employees with good work ethic, training assistance, labor information, human resource services, employment-related services that reduce difficulties on the job

- Other community agencies
  A dependable partner that brings resources to the table
  Good communicator
  Employment specialist with strong ties to employer community
  Leader in development of integrated systems
  Provider of funding for education and training
- Schools and training institutions
  On-site partner that is integrated into employment-related instruction
  Provider of funding
  Link to employment community
  Focus on at-risk students
- Private funders
  Leadership and innovative action on welfare-to-work issues
  Accountability, results
- Economic development organizations (added as supporting customer at board's second group discussion; following is what board believes is valued)
  Quality workforce
  Partner in assessing labor market
  Human resource services

G. Whether the Organization Is Successful and in What Ways

- STARS is highly successful based on performance standards of government funders
- STARS is highly successful in building the confidence and motivation of primary customers
- STARS has been highly successful in bringing government funding for employment services to the area
- STARS is moderately successful at delivering what employers value
- STARS is highly-to-moderately successful as a partner to community agencies and educational institutions but is looked to for a stronger leadership role
- STARS has not been successful in a key area of referral to dependable job placement agencies—the chief complaint of primary customers
- STARS is highly successful at attracting and retaining a professional and committed staff
- STARS has been moderately-to-not-at-all successful at communicating its presence and value to service area communities
- STARS has not been successful in looking to sources of funds beyond government contracts

Exhibit 10 (continued)

H. What Results Should Be

- Continue to exceed government contract performance standards
- People receiving public assistance develop long-term economic self-sufficiency
- Youth develop employment skills, a positive work ethic, and make smooth school-to-work transitions
- Primary customers gain increased skills and confidence that enable them to obtain jobs and advance their careers in their chosen fields
- Employers regard STARS as a valued partner in developing and retaining a qualified workforce
- Increased training/retraining opportunities
- To become the recognized area leader in employment and training activities
- To strengthen the overall economy and cohesiveness of area communities
- To strengthen the organization financially

I. Programs That Should Be Strengthened, Abandoned, or Analyzed

- Core assessment and counseling program should be strengthened to allow greater amount of time working on goals and plans with each participant
- Initial in-take appointments should be available within twenty-four hours of customer request; counselors should be available on campus at colleges and training institutions
- Enhance "cultural competence" to be more effective with diverse customers
- Follow-up should occur beyond ninety days currently required; ongoing service should be available
- Fee-for-service and alternatively funded programs for currently "non-eligible" participants should be explored
- Relationships with employers should be strengthened with more follow-up; fee-for-service options should be explored
- Relationship with job placement agencies should be analyzed and improved or abandoned, with development of such services internally if necessary
- Staff time for development of partnerships and collaborations should be analyzed and increased if necessary

J. Internal Systems That Should Be Assessed

- Financial accounting—currently only set up to manage government contracts
- Public relations and marketing
- Hours and locations of services; staff scheduling
- Grantseeking and other means of financial development
- Board and staff development

K. Draft Goals

All suggestions:

- Expand employment services to serve expanded definition of primary customer
- Enhance our services so they are more "life-changing," so impact is more than a quick fix
- Become a community service agency as opposed to a government service agency
- Demonstrate effective new approaches to employment
- Become a more highly valued partner of the business community
- Establish services to employers and make money doing it
- Demonstrate a positive track record with current welfare-to-work and school-to-work efforts and increase impact in these areas
- Be the leader in transition to employment
- Increase and diversity funding
- Enhance board composition and skills and develop our staff
- Become much better known and understood in the region

Agreement on five goals:

- Expand range of employment services and actively market them to all primary customers.
- Develop and market valued services to employers as a "business venture."
- Take a leadership role in regional employment and training initiatives.*
- Develop a broader funding base and build reserves.
- Strengthen board composition, staff skills, and organizational marketing ability.

*Based on draft goals at this point in the self-assessment process, the executive director submits a proposal for the current grants cycle of the Regional Grantmakers Futures Fund, a funding collaborative encouraging innovation in welfare-to-work initiatives.

Completing the Plan

Phase Three in the self-assessment process is devoted to finalizing your organization's mission and crafting the plan. New participants may yet join the process; people likely to have a role in carrying out objectives and action steps are invited to take part in developing them. The Assessment Team meets frequently in Phase Three to confirm goals and results, to review management's objectives and budget, and to shape the final plan for presentation to the board. Formal self-assessment concludes with the opportunity to evaluate how the process has deepened your sense of purpose, helped clarify your goals, and proven to be an adventure in organizational self-discovery. The five steps in Phase Three are as follows:

1. Revise the mission (if needed); confirm goals and results.
2. Develop objectives, action steps, and budget [management].
3. Prepare the plan for presentation to the board.
4. Present the mission, goals, and supporting budget for board approval.
5. Distribute the plan, confirm responsibilities and dates for initial appraisal.

Overview of Phase Three

Step 1: Revise the mission (if needed); confirm goals and results

If a decision to revise the mission was reached in the second group discussion or retreat, the Assessment Team's first order of business in Phase Three is to revise the mission. The Assessment Team then confirms goals and results and discusses whether a vision statement should be developed. The chief executive gains input on the design of Step 2, and a date is set for the plan to be completed.

Step 2: Develop objectives, action steps, and budgets [management]

In Step 2, management builds understanding and ownership for the emerging plan by involving those who will be responsible for carrying it out in developing objectives, action steps, and the budgets. The chief executive designs and oversees Step 2. Using the mission and goals for direction, the chief executive gives specific assignments to staff and volunteer work groups or task forces. Following an orientation session, the chief executive directs the work groups in the development of draft objectives, action steps, and the budget.

Step 3: Prepare the plan for presentation to the board

The Assessment Team moves through a final review of the plan, makes necessary modifications, prepares a vision statement if one is desired, decides responsibility for appraisal, and prepares the board presentation. The group may wish to set aside time to review its accomplishments or plan a celebration. The board chairman concludes Step 3 by giving final approval of the plan for presentation to the board.

Step 4: Present the mission, goals, and supporting budget for board approval

The board is asked to formally approve the mission, vision (if included), goals, and major allocation of resources. Objectives are presented to the board for information but do not require formal board approval. Self-assessment concludes with approval of the plan and an opportunity for reflection and evaluation.

■ **Step 5: Distribute the plan; confirm responsibilities and dates for initial appraisal**

> Immediately following board approval, the plan is distributed inside the organization. Plan summaries may also be distributed to select outside individuals and groups. Board approval of the plan authorizes the chief executive to begin implementation.

Detailed Steps

STEP 1 Revise the mission (if needed); confirm goals and results

■ **If a new mission statement is needed**

> *If the decision was made at a retreat or second group discussion to revise the mission, the Assessment Team or a special task force is to do the following:*
>
> - Draft a new mission statement.
> - Gain preliminary endorsement of the revised mission from the board chairman *before* confirming goals and results.
> - Propose a revised mission statement for board approval as part of the final plan.
>
> In some cases, developing a new mission statement merely requires fine-tuning of the current statement, and the Assessment Team quickly and easily completes the task. At the other extreme, suggestions for changing the mission go to the very heart of the organization, and in-depth work is essential before meaningful goals can be developed. A detailed process for developing a mission statement is provided in Resource 3. The Assessment Team must exercise its judgment concerning the best approach and timing for developing a revised mission statement.

■ **Confirm goals and results**

> Confirming goals and results is a painstaking process. Groups often bounce back and forth on whether something is a goal, result, objective, or an action step. To review.

- Goals are overarching, limited in number (three to five), and answer the question, *What are the organization's fundamental long-range aims?* Goals are approved by the board.

- Results are the organization's bottom line and are measured in changed lives. They answer the question, *What change in people's behavior, circumstances, health, hopes, competence, or capacity do we intend to achieve?* Results are monitored by the board.

- Objectives are specific and measurable levels of achievement. Objectives answer the question, *What are the major, concrete strategies that management will implement to achieve the organization's goals?* Objectives are presented to the board for information.

- Action steps are the detailed plans and activities to meet objectives. Action steps say who is responsible and when appraisal will occur. Action steps answer the question of *accountability for meeting objectives.* The development of objectives and action steps is management's responsibility.

Immediately following endorsement of a draft mission statement, the Assessment Team holds one or more meetings to confirm goals and results. These are pivotal discussions in the self-assessment process, which must receive proper time and go to sufficient depth. Some Assessment Teams invite a broader group to participate and, especially on the question of appraising results, may look to examples or expertise outside the organization. The writer is part of these sessions, which may be formally facilitated.

The Assessment Team also considers whether to develop a vision statement—a picture of the desired future that may help build understanding and enthusiasm for the plan. Some use a detailed and poetic description of future results—how people with "changed lives" will live. Others decide that no vision statement is necessary, that mission, goals, and objectives speak for themselves. The final decision on whether to include a vision statement is made in Step 3, when the Assessment Team begins preparing the plan for board presentation.

The chief executive's responsibility is to design and lead the process for developing objectives, action steps, and the budget. To conclude Step 1, the chief executive leads a discussion with the Assessment Team to preview the process and gain team members' input and suggestions for moving forward. The Assessment Team then sets a deadline for the draft plan to be ready for presentation to the board.

To complete Step 1, the Assessment Team does the following:

- Reviews the final report and confirms draft goals and results.
- Discusses whether to develop a vision statement.
- Gives input to the chief executive's design for developing objectives, action steps, and budget.
- Sets a completion date for the draft plan.

STEP 2 Develop objectives, action steps, and budget [management]

This step accomplishes four things:

- Management builds understanding and ownership for the emerging plan.
- Work groups draft concrete measurable objectives and put them to a "reality test" by thinking through what will be required to meet them.
- Work groups develop draft action steps, assign responsibility for implementation, and set dates for appraisal.
- Necessary resources are determined, and draft budget is developed.

Design the process

The chief executive provides leadership to design and oversee this step. He or she has final responsibility for objectives and action steps and, together with the board chairman, prepares a supporting budget to present to the full board for approval.

Development of draft objectives, action steps, and budgets may be assigned to existing staff work groups, to special task forces, or to individuals. Assessment Team members and others may be asked to lead work groups or task forces. A facilitator may, if called for, assist individual work groups or task forces.

Make assignments

Mission and goals provide the strategic direction for developing objectives. The number of work groups or task forces and their specific assignments vary depending on the size and structure of the organization and the unique elements of each self-assessment process and plan. The immediate question is *What will be management's specific concrete strategies to reach the goals and achieve results?* The organization has documented a wealth of information from the environmental scan, internal data, customer research, and the insights of self-assessment participants that can be used to help develop objectives.

To make assignments, the chief executive does the following:

- Reviews self-assessment findings and reports.
- Considers the scope of each goal.
- Determines how possible objectives can be clustered together for development.
- Sets on a reasonable number of clear assignments.
- Thinks through the best match with people's understanding, responsibility,

and expertise.

- Determines a leader for each work group or task force that will develop draft objectives, action steps, and budget.

Involve those who will be accountable

To build understanding and ownership for the plan, people who will be accountable for meeting objectives and carrying out action steps must develop them. This includes staff and operational volunteers responsible for particular programs, together with people who work across the organization in areas such as program, finance, field, information systems, communications, human resources, and other specializations.

When the chief executive has made assignments, work group or task force leaders then have the responsibility to:

A. Involve others in accordance with guidelines established by the chief executive.
B. Produce draft objectives, action steps, dates for appraisal, and budget within the established format and time frame.
C. Facilitate the process or coordinate with a facilitator.
D. Work with the chief executive to finalize budget.
E. Serve as a communications liaison for their group.

Work groups or task forces that develop draft objectives, action steps, and budget need clear direction, a deadline, and management support. Although not a member of every group, the chief executive leads this process and should directly contribute his or her insights, monitor progress, and provide encouragement and assistance as necessary.

Questions for developing objectives, action steps, and budget

The following questions provide a structured guide for developing objectives, action steps, and budget:

1. Is the goal clear and commonly understood?
2. What strategies could lead to achieving the goal?
3. What are the pros and cons of each option?
4. What is the best course of action?
5. What are the major, concrete steps to take?
6. Who will be responsible for carrying them out?
7. What are the measures of progress and achievement?
8. When should performance be appraised?

9. What human and financial resources are necessary?
10. How will these resources be developed?

Work groups and task forces can answer these questions through review of self-assessment reports, in group discussions, and, when necessary, by obtaining information or expert input from outside the organization.

Five Elements of Effective Plans: A Summary

Abandonment. The first planning decision is abandonment of what does not work, what has never worked—the things that have outlived their usefulness and their capacity to contribute. Ask of any program, system, or customer group, "If we were not committed to this today, would we go into it?" If the answer is no, say, "How can we get out—fast?"

Concentration is building on success, strengthening what *does* work. When you have strong performance is the very time to ask, "Can we set an even higher standard?" Concentration is vital, but it's also very risky. You must chose the right concentrations, or you leave your flanks totally uncovered.

Innovation. You must look for tomorrow's success, the true innovations, the diversity that stirs the imagination. What are the opportunities? Do they fit you? Do you really believe in this? But you have to be careful. Before you go into something new, don't say, "This is how we do it." Say, "Let's find out what this requires."

Risk taking. There is the risk you can afford to take— if it goes wrong, it is easily reversible with minor damage. And there are decisions where the risk is great but you cannot afford *not* to take it. You have to balance the short range with the long. If you are too conservative, you miss the opportunity. If you commit too much too fast, there may not be a long run to worry about.

Analysis. Finally, it is important to recognize when you do *not* know, when you are not yet sure whether to abandon, concentrate or go into something new—or if a particular risk is necessary. Then your objective is to conduct an analysis.

Hold an orientation session

An orientation session is helpful to work group or task force leaders and, indeed, to all who will participate in this step. At the orientation session:

- The chief executive provides an overview of developing objectives, action steps, and budget.

- Self-assessment reports are briefly summarized and noted as an important resource to draw from and build upon.
- Mission, goals, and results are reviewed and discussed.
- Peter Drucker's comments on effective plans from the Participant Workbook are reviewed and discussed (see box).
- Work group and task force assignments, process, and deadlines are discussed to ensure understanding and agreement.

To conclude Step 2, work groups or task forces submit completed drafts to the chief executive, who does the following:

- Reviews objectives and action steps to:
    Find aspects that can be enhanced or combined for greater effectiveness.
    Affirm measures of progress and achievement or suggest changes.
    Recommend changes in timing so the overall plan flows well.
    Suggest other modifications or additions.
- Reviews the emerging plan to confirm it effectively addresses:
    Abandonment
    Concentration
    Innovation
    Risk taking
    Analysis
- Affirms dates for appraisal or suggests modifications.
- Conveys feedback and suggested modifications to group leaders and, when necessary, requests second drafts.
- Provides encouragement and support to leaders and groups as they complete their task.

STEP 3   Prepare the plan for presentation to the board

Focus on content over structure

When the chief executive leads the development of the final plan, it is important that content not be overshadowed by structure. Writing vision statements, goals, and objectives is not an exact science, nor is the final language of any two plans exactly the same. Wording may require considerable attention to thoroughly capture the organization's overarching direction and succinctly present management's objectives. It is quite common for groups to "work the plan up and down" more than once before settling on a final draft.

Integrate appraisal

Appraisal is ongoing. It includes monitoring progress and achievement and making necessary modifications to the plan. It is essential for appraisal to be integrated into existing board and management practices. Some organizations also form a committee to appraise progress and achievement overall or to review specific objectives.

The chief executive and Assessment Team hold final meetings and do the following:

- Accept recommended objectives, action steps, and budget or make final modifications.
- Make a final decision about whether a vision statement will be included in the plan.
- Decide responsibility for appraisal.
- Determine to whom and in what form the plan will be distributed (see Step 5).
- Discuss how presenting the plan to the board will be handled. Considerations are as follows:

  Whether others will assist the chairman and chief executive in presenting the plan and responding to questions

  What is sufficient time for discussion and formal approval

  What the role of the facilitator is, if one is used

  How suggestions to modify the plan will be handled

  What the formal process for approval is

  How self-assessment participants will be recognized

- Confirm a deadline with the writer to prepare a plan summary to include:

  The current or newly drafted mission statement

  A vision statement (if called for)

  Goals

  Objectives

  A summary budget

  A description of how appraisal will occur

- Endorse a final version of the plan.

At the final meeting of the Assessment Team, the group may wish to set aside time to review its accomplishments or plan a celebration. The board chairman concludes Step 3 by giving final approval of the plan that will be presented to the

---

board.

STEP 4   Present the mission, goals, and supporting budget for board approval

The plan is presented at a regular or specially convened meeting of the board. The vision (if included), mission, goals, objectives, and budget summary are sent in advance. The summary, verbal presentation, and discussion provide a view of the overall plan. However, the board is asked to formally approve only the mission, vision, goals, and major allocation of resources. Responsibility for appraisal is reviewed. Objectives, while presented for information, do not require board approval. They are the responsibility of management. Action steps are not presented to the board.

Approval of the plan signals conclusion of self-assessment as a distinct undertaking and provides the opportunity for reflection and evaluation. Board members may be asked to discuss ways in which the self-assessment process

- Went well or could have been improved.
- Deepened their sense of purpose.
- Helped clarify goals.
- Has been an adventure in organizational self-discovery.

STEP 5   Distribute the plan; confirm responsibilities and dates for initial appraisal

Immediately following board approval, the plan is distributed throughout the organization. This may include a written summary as well as presentations for staff and volunteers. Plan summaries may also go to individuals outside the organization who participated in the environmental scan or customer research. Some groups find it valuable to publish a well-designed summary for wide distribution, and many use their plan as an attachment to, or the basis for, funding and partnership proposals.

Board approval of the plan authorizes the chief executive to begin implementation. The board continues to carry responsibility for appraisal, oversight, and review. The organization's focus turns to action—and to results.

PART THREE

Resources for Self-Assessment

Uses of the Drucker *Self-Assessment Tool:* Four Examples

- Using Self-Assessment to Reinvigorate a Project

- Asking "What Is Our Mission?" as Orientation for New Members of the Board

- Using Self-Assessment as a Guide to New Program Development

- Putting Theory into Practice: Self-Assessment as a University Teaching Tool and Field Project Guide

Four examples will show how the *Self-Assessment Tool* can be adapted and used for a number of purposes, in addition to a comprehensive organizational self-assessment process. Each case example describes a situation, provides a sample process, and reports outcomes of using the *Tool* in this manner. The cases are:

1. Using self-assessment to reinvigorate a project
2. Asking "What Is Our Mission?" as orientation for new members of the board
3. Using self-assessment as a guide to new program development
4. Putting theory into practice: self-assessment as a university teaching tool and field project guide

Using self-assessment to reinvigorate a project

Situation

The excitement within the Research Initiatives Committee has worn off. Two years earlier, this physician-led group succeeded in gaining a commitment from their affiliated national public health organization to raise $25 million to launch a new round of studies the committee felt would lead to a bona fide breakthrough in the treatment of a debilitating disease, perhaps even a cure. Some promising projects were launched, but the committee was bogged down with the idea of establishing regional centers for research; a leading institution was to be a partner in coordinating a group of studies and linking them in a national system.

Money is coming in slowly; the proper geographic distribution of the centers is in continuous debate; and committee leaders have become convinced that the roles of two crucial partners—federal research institutes and pharmaceutical foundations—have been woefully underdeveloped. The new idea is to call a "summit meeting" of all the potential partners and develop a fresh understanding of how to move forward. A facilitator is engaged to help plan the summit; after being briefed, he suggests the committee would benefit from an abbreviated self-assessment process. The committee chairman is worried about wasting more time. "This looks like ground we've been over. I've got the committee coming in from around the country, and we've only got half a day to get a plan for the summit. The questions look awfully basic. Will this get us where we need to go?" With further conversation, it is decided that government and industry representatives will be invited to the planning meeting, and the chairman agrees that taking one step back might be the best way to get two steps forward.

Process Design

Objective: Develop a plan for a "partners summit" that will result in regained momentum toward breakthrough research. Starting date is March 1.

Step	Who's Responsible	By When
1. Expand invitations to May 1 Research Initiatives Committee meeting to include a government and industry representative and provide advance orientation.	Chairman, staff	ASAP
2. Develop tight meeting agenda with sufficient time to:	Facilitator, chairman, staff	4/1

• Affirm the mission of the research initiative.

• Confirm the primary customer and what the committee believes they value.

• Confirm supporting customers and what the committee believes they value.

• Determine what is still to be learned from customers.

• Confirm objectives for a productive summit and assign action steps.

3. Send agenda and Participant Workbooks to attendees with instructions to complete Worksheets 1, 4, 5, 7, 8, and 12 in advance of the meeting.	Staff	4/10
4. Conduct meeting.	Staff, facilitator	5/1
5. Deliver report to chairman.	Staff, facilitator	5/5

Outcome

The meeting is a success, but the outcome—canceling the summit in favor of another approach—is a surprise. The discussions on mission, the primary customer, beliefs about what they value, and what results should be go quickly and smoothly. The clear focus of the research initiative is to make discoveries that will lead to vastly improved quality of life for patients, an end to deaths caused by this disease, and possible prevention of the disease altogether in the long run. Once this point in the agenda is reached, a committee member comments: "It's

---

remarkable. I think we had begun to see our mission as getting these damn centers off the ground rather than curing a disease."

The discussion on supporting customers is longer and more difficult. Having government and industry representatives in the room helps bridge the gap between assumptions about customer value and what real customers have to say. This is the turning point. Committee members realize they have allowed one supporting customer group—the regional caucuses in the national organization—to drive the partnership design. When they listen to the different possibilities of including industry and government as equal partners, they see the potential to further the mission faster and much more effectively than through trying to maintain a new regional system.

The decision to cancel the summit comes from the realization that it is premature. A great deal more needs to be learned from supporting customers. The committee develops a list of eighteen specific customers and a preliminary list of questions to ask them; the committee agrees to take on in-person interviews, then come back in sixty days and redesign the initiative based on what roles their potential partners truly value and would actively take on. The chairman's summation: "It isn't what I had in mind . . . it feels a bit like starting over. But I see it as the right track and I believe we'll finally get on the road to what I signed up for in the first place, which is some results that can make a difference for my patients."

Asking "What is our mission?" as orientation for new members of the board

Situation

The leadership team of a suburban county library is preparing to welcome four new members to its citizen-elected board—a 50 percent turnover in the group. The board chairman recalls her introduction to the board to have been "pretty traditional. We studied library rules and regulations and saw a lot of statistics. I did enjoy the aspect of our orientation that explained how we would handle demands to ban books, but there was something lacking. It was detail without a more significant context. This board took a long time to get to what I consider our central role of stewardship of the institution's mission." The library director suggests that can be the very place for orientation to begin. An Internet search identifies the *Self-Assessment Tool* as a resource and, upon reviewing the materials, the director and board chairman agree to its use.

Process Design

Objective: Provide an orientation session for new and existing board members that develops genuine understanding and appreciation for the library's mission.

Step	Who's Responsible	By When
1. Confirm session date with all board members and see to logistics.	Director	ASAP
2. Conduct "mini" environmental scan and develop report.	Director and staff	Week 4
3. Gather and synthesize internal data and recent patron survey results.	Director and staff	Week 4
4. Engage and orient internal facilitator for session.	Director	Week 5
5. Meet with facilitator to confirm session purpose and develop agenda.	Leadership team	Week 5
6. Send to board members: • Participant Workbook • Report of scan, the synthesized data, and survey results • Cover letter, including session purpose, agenda, and instructions, in order to review Preface, Introduction, and discussion of "What Is Our Mission?" and complete Worksheets 1–4.	Director	Week 6
7. Conduct session.	Facilitator	Week 7
8. Evaluate session.	Leadership team	Week 8

Outcome

Every member of the board rates the session as *Excellent* or *Very Good* in the evaluation. A first-time member comments, "Not only did I get to know the library better, I appreciated the immediate opportunity for a meaningful exchange with my new colleagues." The director is specially pleased at what she personally gained from the extensive preparation: "Our mission is *to enrich people's lives with information and cultural resources.* I actually decided to write the environmental scan report myself because I saw it as a rare opportunity to draw together so many important trends my staff and I are exposed to in our professional circles and every day on the front lines. There is certainly nothing staid about the field today!

We are very much caught up in the information revolution. I feel clearer about our purpose and direction as a result of this exercise, and that makes me a better leader." The board chairman concludes, "This was certainly among the most substantive discussions I have had on the board. I believe I have learned that mission should always be the place we start."

Using self-assessment as a guide to new program development

Situation

A United Way announces a communitywide request for proposals for innovative strategies to "develop the physical and emotional health of every child in the early years." United Way leaders decide to distribute the *Self-Assessment Tool* as a guide to proposal development and award up to eight short-term planning grants based on a preliminary goal and self-assessment process design. Three potentially renewable funding contracts will then be awarded to groups proposing the most compelling initiatives.

A three-way partnership between a community clinic, an HMO, and an anti-smoking group receives a planning grant to fully develop its concept for a health promotion strategy with young pregnant women called No Butts About It.

Goal

Nicotine threatens healthy prenatal development, and secondhand smoke poses a danger to young lungs. Yet no community health program specifically targets young pregnant women with a concentrated effort to help them quit smoking. No Butts About It will help protect the basic health and well-being of children in their early years and reduce the ill effects of smoking on their mothers and families. The initiative's goal: *to reduce smoking among pregnant women and promote a smoke-free environment for their children.*

Process Design

Objective: Develop a self-assessment report and plan that gains United Way support for No Butts About It.

Step	Who's Responsible	By When
1. Establish an Assessment Team (A-Team) with representatives from each partner organization.	Chief execs	Month 1
2. Interview and select a facilitator, writer, and research consultant.	Chief execs, A-Team	Month 1
3. Prior to initial meeting, A-Team facilitator and writer receive background on United Way request for proposals (RFP) process, background research and information on "No Butts" goal, and self-assessment Participant Workbook with instructions to complete Worksheets 3, 5, 7, 8, and 9.	Chief execs	Month 1
4. At its initial meeting, the A-Team: • Reviews United Way RFP, "No Butts" background research and goal. • Answers "What are our opportunities?" • Defines primary and supporting customers. • Determines beliefs on customer value. • Discusses what knowledge the team would like to gain about the primary and supporting customers. • Makes preliminary commitments to participate in customer research. • Appoints coordinators for customer research. • Sets dates for upcoming meetings.	Facilitator, A-Team	Month 2
5. Customer research is designed.	Coordinators, research consultant	Month 2
6. A-Team meets to confirm customer research design and individual assignments.	A-Team, research consultant	Month 2
7. Customer research conducted; report developed and distributed.	A-Team, research consultant, writer, others as identified	Month 3–4

Step	Who's Responsible	By When
8. Customer research briefing is held with A-Team, chief executives, facilitator, and writer.	Coordinators, research consultant	Month 4
9. Prior to next meeting, A-Team completes Worksheets 12, 15, and 16 in the Participant Workbook.	A-Team	Month 5
10. A-Team holds three to five meetings to: • Confirm the initiative's goal. • Define what results should be. • Determine objectives. • Develop an action plan and budget.	A-Team, facilitator, writer	Month 5–6
11. Complete first draft of final report and plan.	Writer	Month 6
12. Meet to review and amend report. and plan.	A-Team, facilitator, writer, chief execs	Month 6
13. Approve report and plan and submit to United Way.	Chief execs	Month 6

Outcome

Self-assessment brings about significantly changed assumptions regarding the goal of No Butts About It and what results should be. Members of the A-Team report an experience that "really challenged our thinking" and helped them work through critical details in the partnership and propose what all consider a "stronger program than we would have had." The final plan flows from a modified goal: *to reduce smoking-related illness among young children.* There are four objectives:

1. Enable pregnant women to reduce their smoking.
2. Increase young mothers' ability to protect their children from secondhand smoke.
3. Develop preventive pediatric care relationships.
4. Sustain a successful service delivery partnership.

   Desired results are:

   • Participants reduce their smoking during pregnancy; 20 percent quit smoking during pregnancy.

- Participants are aware of the dangers of secondhand smoke; 10 percent of participants maintain a completely smoke-free environment during their baby's first year.
- Participants' babies receive regular first-year check-ups and immunizations; 25 percent have reduced crisis-oriented health care and reduced smoking-related early-childhood illnesses.

Assessment Team members describe how a major shift happened in the process. "It came from really getting to know these young women," reflects the HMO representative. "Many are highly motivated to quit smoking while they're pregnant. They've gotten the message on that, and it's important for them to try to do the right thing for their baby. That's what will bring them in. But when we really got down to it, we thought, 'Wouldn't it be wonderful if we could help them to *stay* in.' There are so many challenges once the baby is born, and so many of these young women disappear off our radar." The community clinic director adds, "This program will be another way for us to establish a strong relationship at the community level. When a young mother trusts us and allows us into her life, we can help see to the basics and introduce her to peer support and so many things that prevent future problems."

The United Way agrees with their approach and awards funding to the initiative. The final report and plan also include a table on health care cost savings when early childhood crisis care and smoking-related illness are reduced. No Butts About It would more than pay for itself on that basis, while bringing young women into an ongoing relationship that could benefit their babies as well as themselves.

Putting theory into practice—self-assessment as a university teaching tool and field project guide

Situation

An adjunct professor is preparing a new semester of an M.B.A. course, "Organizational Management and Leadership." She is looking for a way to augment her teaching plan so students can deepen their understanding through a direct field experience. Upon reviewing the *Self-Assessment Tool*, she believes it is the type of analytical guide she has been looking for but is uncertain if it can be adapted for use with business as well as nonprofit organizations. "I was attracted by the clarity of the core principles," she reports. "When I reviewed other Drucker work on management, I could see parallel applications to business and government as well as nonprofits. The *Tool* seemed to answer my need for a theoretical framework combined with a structure to apply it."

Process Design

Objective: Students gain understanding of organizational planning and performance by conducting field projects using the *Self-Assessment Tool.*

Step	*By When*
1. Students complete assigned readings on planning, management, process facilitation, evaluation and measurement, and leading change. Field project assignment introduced and discussed.	Week 1
2. Class discussion on identifying client organizations, determining the organization's purpose in undertaking self-assessment, developing the process design and steps in "contracting" with the organization. Students assigned to begin keeping personal journal with reflections on field project.	Week 2
3. Students, working in pairs, identify client organizations and submit their proposed process design and contract with the organization for critique and approval.	Week 3
4. Students submit first progress report. Class discussion on issues and challenges in facilitating organizational planning.	Week 6
5. Students submit paper, "Factors That Encourage and Inhibit Organizational Change and Performance," incorporating observations from the projects to date.	Week 8
6. Individual tutorials held on field projects.	Week 8–10
7. Students submit second progress report. Class discussion on developing plans and ensuring effective implementation.	Week 11
8. Students submit final project report and summary of personal journal reflections.	Week 14
9. Projects and reflections presented, discussed, and evaluated in class.	Week 14–16

Outcome

Twenty-six students register for the course (nearly twice the predicted number), and all complete self-assessment projects: one with a government agency, two at universities, six with nonprofit organizations, and six with businesses. All students gather data, facilitate meetings, deliver feedback to their clients, and write final reports; however, the projects tend to emphasize one or another aspect of self-assessment as opposed to full self-assessment processes. Students assist their client organizations by helping to clarify missions, leading focus groups with customers, developing objectives regarding fundraising and board development, and, in all cases, helping develop action plans that, in the judgment of the instructor, "would make the organizations more effective in the community or the business world." Class presentations and discussion allow students to benefit from each others' experience and gain a more holistic perspective.

Student evaluations nearly all rate the course among "the best I have taken." Most highly valued by the students are the "real-world relationships" that take place while finding a client, contracting with a client, and practicing group facilitation. They discover that "planning and performance are as much about relationships with people as they are about delivering a product." And they learn more about themselves. Writes one, "This experience has been the most important motivating factor in helping me determine what I want to pursue once I graduate from the M.B.A. program." The instructor concludes, "Students walked away from this course with their eyes open wider about real organizational dynamics. They put theory into practice and learned a structure for analysis that they should be able to use again and again."

Effective Facilitation

"There is, in fact, only one legitimate source of pleasure in chairmanship, and that is pleasure in the achievements of the meeting—and to be legitimate, it must be shared by all those present."

Antony Jan, "How to Run a Meeting,"
Harvard Business Review, March-April 1976

Effective facilitation is an art. It requires advance preparation, a well-structured agenda, and the prudent use of group dynamics techniques. It requires looking and listening, feeding back observations, exercising disciplined neutrality, and being able to improvise. The facilitator is at once leader and follower—there to guide a group and there to be flexible in whatever way best serves it.

Facilitation is complex because history, culture, circumstances, and personalities differ in every organization and in every group. Yet positive evaluations of group discussions or retreats consistently cite the same factors: we stayed on time, on task, and there was a positive dynamic that encouraged our best contributions. The root meaning of the word *facilitate* is *render easy,* and that is what effective facilitation does. No matter how challenging or difficult a meeting's subject matter, participation is rendered easy.

Neutrality

The distinction between facilitation and other types of group leadership is the facilitator's neutrality. The facilitator is responsible for process rather than content. The moment he or she is perceived to be advancing a point of view, credibility is damaged and trust in the process diminished. Group members often put facilitators to the test in this regard, and internal facilitators must be specially alert to put aside their own opinions and demonstrate objectivity. On occasion, the facilitator may have command of facts or insights of value to the group that no one else has cited. In such cases—and this is always a risk—facilitators may temporarily "step out of role" and contribute their comments but then must clearly demonstrate objectivity with regard to the group's response.

Facilitator tip: When a group seeks your opinion, first ask, "What do you think?" Many times participants can answer their own questions. This encourages contribution and protects your neutrality.

Effective facilitation also calls for objectivity in monitoring and providing feedback on the group's interactions. Here, the effective facilitator helps participants take responsibility for their own contribution and for the dynamics of the group as a whole. If a facilitator says, "I think we are stuck because you are not really listening to each other," the facilitator becomes both judge and jury. By asking instead, "Are people feeling stuck?" and following with "What will help us to move forward?" the facilitator is asking participants to judge the situation for themselves.

Objectivity requires conscious practice. Even the most seasoned facilitator will sometimes slip out of neutral, but such mistakes are generally forgiven when promptly acknowledged. The subject matter of group discussions, retreats, and other self-assessment meetings is compelling, and the temptation to contribute is great. The facilitator's pleasure must not be in hearing his or her own voice but in encouraging the voices of others.

> ***Facilitator tip:*** *Before beginning every group session, review the objectives and take a moment to commit yourself to being neutral and serving the needs of the group.*

Authority

The facilitator's role as process leader is a strong one. Participants expect the facilitator to have a firm grasp of the agenda, the organization's decision-making protocols, and how session objectives will be reached. Participants depend on the facilitator to help create an open atmosphere and to intervene with difficult individuals or if the group as a whole veers off track. Nonetheless, the facilitator's authority to carry out this leadership role cannot be automatically assumed nor can it be conferred from above. Authority is given by the group itself.

The facilitator's first task is to help the group set ground rules—a set of points that all agree will help ensure the most productive session. The facilitator also confirms specifically what is desired of him or her in the facilitation role, which creates a compact with the group. If ground rules are violated, the facilitator is authorized to call this to the group's attention. If the group has asked that no one be allowed to dominate, the facilitator can request that a long winded participant yield the floor. Once ground rules are spelled out, the facilitator's authority to lead the process becomes legitimate and is likely to be supported. Nearly every group can easily define what makes for a good meeting, and most participants welcome even firm reminders of such guidelines.

> ***Facilitator tip:*** *Once the group has given you authority, use it.*

Time

The careful allotment and tracking of time is critical to a successful meeting. This is partly a matter of developing appropriate objectives and a sensible agenda, but rarely does a group proceed exactly as planned. Here, effective facilitation requires both precision and flexibility.

The facilitator should announce the time allotments for particular discussion items or exercises, inform people of minutes remaining, and make every attempt to keep on schedule. However, the exact timing of each agenda item is not so important as following the natural flow of discussion that develops. The facilitator should always be prepared to extend or curtail time allowed, rearrange agenda items or modify planned exercises, and, if it appears the group cannot cover the agenda in sufficient depth and still run on time, the facilitator must stop the group briefly and gain a decision on how best to proceed.

Facilitator tip: *Work for timing that matches the group's best pace. Never rush through an important point; it will only resurface later.*

Encouraging contribution

Active contribution is ultimately the responsibility of each self-assessment participant, yet a great deal can be done to encourage it. People enter into group discussions in their own way and at their own pace. Encouragement first requires a structure for discussion that engages people across many differing styles:

- Confident public speakers in any size group vs. those who more easily contribute in small groups or pairs
- People who discover their thoughts through conversation vs. by quiet musing, writing, or drawing
- Eager volunteers vs. participants who seldom speak unless directly called upon
- Those able to voice their opinions moment to moment vs. those who require time to reflect

The sample annotated agendas in the text provide examples of varied structures that facilitate discussion. There are groups where such orchestration is essential. And there are groups in which discussion flows so naturally that anything but minimal structure gets in the way. The general rule is to offer variety, but, here again, the facilitator must be willing to throw aside even the best-laid plans and concentrate on the approaches that work with a particular group.

Facilitator tip: *Prepare more structure than you need, have a few back-up ideas, and be ready to give up all of it.*

Equal in importance to a flexible structure is the facilitator's skill at moderating discussion. The effective facilitator sees who is quick to comment and who is reticent, notes body language and nonverbal signs, monitors how well participants appear to understand one another, and works to balance contribution and involvement across the group. A good facilitator senses when to limit discussion and when to draw it out, and employs moderating techniques such as the following:

- Remaining silent and giving participants time to add to what has just been said.
- Turning key words into questions: "What about it is interesting?" or "In what way would it be challenging?"
- Requesting that someone recap a preceding point to ensure understanding, then requesting further responses from the group.
- Calling on quiet group members: "[Name], we haven't heard from you on this; what are your thoughts?"
- Asking a participant to clarify a position: "I'm a little confused. Earlier you said this; now I believe I'm hearing you say that."
- Using humor. A good joke can warm up a crowd.
- Thanking and positively reinforcing individual contributors and the group as a whole.
- Either encouraging or limiting contribution with phrases such as:

  What do you mean when you say . . . ?

  I'm not sure I understand. Could you restate the comment in another way?

  What are some of your reasons for feeling that way?

  I hear that you disagree. Can you make an alternative suggestion?

  Tell us more about your thinking on that issue.

  [Name], you've already spoken a number of times. Let's hear from someone who hasn't.

  We'll have more time on this issue later in the agenda. Let's save additional comments until then.

  Thank you. Others?

  Can you give an example?

  Those are excellent points. What do others think?

  It appears there is agreement. Let's move on.

Constructive dissent

Constructive dissent—the open expression of honest disagreement—is vital to productive discussion and sound decision making. As Peter Drucker points out, "If you have quick consensus on an important matter, don't make the decision. Acclamation means nobody has done the homework. And open discussion uncovers what the objections are. With genuine participation, a decision doesn't need to be sold. Suggestions can be incorporated, objections addressed, and the decision itself becomes a commitment to action."

The encouragement of constructive dissent should be cited—by the facilitator if necessary—as a ground rule. Some groups naturally warm to it, but when there is hesitancy, the facilitator must draw dissent out. Reluctance may stem from a negative history that makes participants feel unsafe, a culture in which dissent is considered impolitic or impolite, or the simple lack of practice. Facilitators cannot overturn history or ignore culture but can, through attentive moderating, ensure that self-assessment discussions are a safe forum. If the facilitator notes the absence of dissent, one may directly ask how it can be encouraged. And if constructive dissent is simply unfamiliar territory, the facilitator can model it by example, set up a dissent role-play exercise, or employ other creative techniques to increase participants' comfort.

Facilitator tip: Your ease, confidence, and readiness to draw out dissent encourages the group.

When dissent comes into the open, it may spark a certain tension or raw edge in the group. To keep dissent constructive, the effective facilitator:

- Encourages the group to listen fully to each person's comments without interrupting.
- Reinforces that participants can voice differing opinions without anyone being "wrong."
- Gains numerous responses to help the group thoroughly air a subject and make the most informed judgment.
- Thanks individual contributors in turn and compliments the group for doing well with dissent.
- Does not allow one or more highly opinionated participants to "railroad" the group.
- May close a subject with agreement to disagree, leaving it to the Assessment Team to decide whether to pursue the matter.

Managing conflict

Conflict in a group is rarely constructive, the way vigorous dissent can be. In conflict, people have become self-righteous, and discussion veers from *what* is right to *who* is right. It is destructive to the group process because people stop listening to each other; they become silent, defensive, or combative, and discussion closes down. Conflict is not necessarily a disaster. Some groups become stronger once it is aired, but it is a distraction that always saps valuable energy and time.

The attentive facilitator may be able to defuse a potential conflict before it starts. However, there are circumstances in which conflict must be allowed to surface and occasions when it erupts seemingly out of nowhere. Then the facilitator must carefully manage the group's dynamics. First, facilitators must resist the reflex to immediately stop a conflict. Those who are engaged need at least a few moments to get it out of their system. This also increases the possibility people will see how they are affecting the group's dynamics and moderate themselves. If you step in too soon, it can become a power struggle with the facilitator. Physically move slightly *toward* people in conflict rather than away. This gives assurance the facilitator is not intimidated.

Next, one quickly takes control of the situation. This may be an emphatic, "Excuse me," to cut short an argument or the first words to break an awkward silence. It is then the facilitator's responsibility to help move the group back to constructive exchange. There are a number of choices. The facilitator may think it best to:

- Ignore the conflict and simply continue on.
- Suggest the group move to another subject and return to this one later.
- Call a short break and confer with the parties involved.
- Acknowledge the strong feelings being expressed and ask those involved to attempt to continue on within the framework of constructive dissent.
- State what the facilitator is hearing as the underlying substance of the conflict and ask the group to speak to it—an important issue may have been exposed that shouldn't be lost.
- Attempt to mediate the conflict but only if this will be in the best interests of the group as a whole and if the facilitator is an experienced mediator.
- Provide an early opportunity for those who have been part of the conflict to make a positive contribution in the group.

There is no formula for making the best choice. The facilitator must make it based on instinct and knowledge of the group. Those not directly involved look to the facilitator to ensure that things don't spin out of control. Those party to the conflict need time to calm down and may appreciate private follow-up. If participants wish to apologize or otherwise acknowledge their behavior in the group, the facilitator should provide this opportunity. Finally, some conflict is best defused with a touch of humor. A facilitator takes a risk with this, but it can be the shortest route back to a positive tone.

Facilitator tip: Should conflict erupt, watch and listen carefully, then quickly make your choice as to how to manage it.

The self-assessment process leads participants to the very heart of an organization, why it exists, and how it will make a difference. This shared exploration is central to creating broad ownership of a plan and the dispersed leadership necessary to carry it out. Group discussions themselves are enriching, but what is finally most important is that people come away able to say, *"We really got somewhere."*

Meetings are work. If preparation is poor or leadership lax, they often seem a waste of time. When both are sound, the process and product can be exhilarating. The effective facilitator continually strives to bring about the greatest sense of accomplishment in a group. One monitors where engagement heats up and where it cools, pushes when necessary, encourages the group to stay with a challenge, and keeps bringing focus to the tasks at hand.

Meetings can produce at least four kinds of accomplishment:

1. *Reaching objectives.* This is the first measure of a meeting's effectiveness.
2. *Achieving a breakthrough.* Some groups get stuck in a rut or find certain questions nearly impossible to fathom. There is relief, appreciation—even delight—when new thinking occurs.
3. *Positive group dynamics.* Keeping an open atmosphere and encouraging constructive dissent is a challenge to many groups. Productive discussion is valuable in the moment and builds skills for effective ongoing communication.
4. *Individual contribution and learning.* Organizational and personal self-discovery are closely linked. Both bring about renewed energy, confidence, and commitment.

Effective facilitation renders contribution easy, yet promotes hard work. The rewards are active engagement, a legitimate sense of accomplishment, knowledge that one's participation mattered, and profound pleasure when these are shared by all those present.

How to Develop
a Mission Statement

Mission: Why you do what you do; the organization's reason for being, its purpose. Says what, in the end, you want to be remembered for.

Changing the mission—or creating an organization's first mission statement—is a process of gathering ideas and suggestions for the mission and honing them into a short, sharply focused phrase that meets specific criteria. Peter Drucker says the mission should "fit on a T-shirt," yet a mission statement is not a slogan. It is a precise statement of purpose. Words should be chosen for their meaning rather than beauty, for clarity over cleverness. The best mission statements are plain speech with no technical jargon and no adornments. Like the mission statement of the International Red Cross—"To serve the most vulnerable"—they come right out and say something. In their brevity and simplicity is power.

The work plan to develop a mission statement calls for a writing group to develop a draft statement and recommend it for the board chairman's endorsement, who then proposes the mission statement for approval by the board. Some groups are able to develop a revised mission very quickly, while others conduct the work over a period of weeks or even months. If the mission is being revisited outside a full self-assessment process, the writing group must, at bare minimum, be able to identify the organization or initiative's primary customer and what the goals and results should be. If understanding or agreement is insufficient on these key points, deeper involvement in the self-assessment process is necessary before an effective mission statement can be developed. If the mission is being revisited within a full self-assessment process, Steps 2 to 8 in the following plan may be condensed.

Work Plan for Developing a Mission Statement

Step	Who's Responsible
1. Establish a mission-writing group (may be the Assessment Team). • Choose a facilitator and a writer.	Chief executive
2. At a first meeting of the writing group: • Adopt criteria for an effective mission statement. • Gather ideas and suggestions for first drafts.	Chief executive, facilitator
3. Develop one or more draft statements.	Writer
4. In a second group meeting, judge initial drafts against criteria and suggest revisions or new options.	Writing group, facilitator
5. Develop second drafts.	Writer

Step	Who's Responsible
6. Gain feedback from outside the writing group.	Chief executive, others as assigned
7. Summarize feedback and distribute second drafts and summary to the writing group.	Chief executive, writer
8. In a third group meeting: • Make recommendations for final revisions and propose a draft mission statement for board approval; or • Sum up the status of the process and determine next steps.	Writing group, facilitator
9. Give preliminary endorsement to the proposed mission statement.	Board chairman
10. Present the proposed mission statement for board approval.	Board chairman

Step 1: Establish a mission-writing group

The task of the mission-writing group is to agree on a draft mission statement to be presented to the governance body for approval. The Assessment Team doubles as the writing group, or a special team may be convened. Members should include the chief executive, the board chairman or another representative of the board, a writer, and a manageable number of additional members who represent different parts of the organization and who are keen to take on the task. Having a facilitator is helpful. It can be particularly beneficial if this individual has facilitated other parts of the organization's self-assessment process.

Step 2: Adopt criteria for an effective mission statement; gather ideas and suggestions for first drafts

The "too many cooks spoil the broth" syndrome that besets so many writing groups is substantially avoided by agreeing on a recipe in advance. Prior to a first meeting, writing group members should review Peter Drucker's discussion on mission in the Participant Workbook and Worksheet 4, which contain criteria for an effective mission statement. At a first meeting, the writing group should post these criteria on a flip chart or chalkboard, review them, consider amendments, and adopt the criteria they will use to judge the effectiveness of the mission they are about to develop.

The suggested criteria for an effective mission statement are that it:

- Is short and sharply focused
- Is clear and easily understood
- Defines why we do what we do; why the organization exists
- Does not prescribe means
- Is sufficiently broad
- Provides direction for doing the right things
- Addresses our opportunities
- Matches our competence
- Inspires our commitment
- Says what, in the end, we want to be remembered for

Following the adoption of criteria, the group moves on to ideas and suggestions for the mission statement. This exercise begins with reviewing the suggestions from a self-assessment retreat or second group discussion, then adding to them. (In some cases, suggestions may be in the form of new draft statements and the group can proceed directly to Step 4.) If the mission is being revisited outside a full self-assessment process, the group moves directly to generating new ideas and suggestions. What is important at this point is to develop the widest possible set of options without being overly critical of any. The facilitator records the group's responses. Many idea-generating techniques can be used, including:

- Open brainstorming: any thought or idea is welcome.
- Each group member finishes the sentence, "The mission should be.... "
- Small teams "compete" in a very short time span to draft and nominate the "best" new mission statement.
- Go around the group two or three times asking for the one word that must be in the mission statement.
- Each person quickly draws a picture of the mission, then "shows and tells."

To conclude the exercise, the group:

- Posts and reviews all ideas and suggestions. The facilitator draws a circle around the words or phrases that appear most often.
- Discusses key ideas or themes that must be captured in the new mission statement.
- Discusses key ideas or themes that must not be part of the new mission statement.

Step 3: Develop one or more draft statements.

Following the meeting, the writer—either alone or with a small subgroup—develops drafts of at least *two* possible new mission statements that are distributed before the next meeting.

Step 4: Judge initial drafts against criteria and suggest revisions or new options

The second meeting of the writing group should begin with a discussion of the protocols (outlined next) that will be followed to judge the drafts and make suggestions. People should also be encouraged to "listen between the lines." This step in the process is highly structured, but on more than one occasion, someone in a group offers a comment or phrase that turns out to be the perfect nugget on which to build the new mission statement. If the group has a "Eureka!" moment, go with it.

To judge drafts and make suggestions:

A. The group reviews the criteria for an effective mission statement.
B. The first draft statement is posted on a flip chart or writing board at the front of the group.
C. Group members individually rate the draft as meets, meets somewhat, doesn't meet for each criterion.
D. The facilitator polls and records the group's response for each criterion to determine the overall strengths and weaknesses of the draft.
E. The group first discusses the merits of the draft and then makes specific suggestions for how it might be improved.

Note: The group is not engaging in collective editing or rewriting. All suggestions—even if they contradict one another—are encouraged and recorded.

F. The second draft statement is posted, and steps C-E are repeated.
G. The group compares and contrasts its reactions to the two drafts.
H. The facilitator instructs each group member to be ready to write, then gives the group two minutes to individually write their recommended mission statement at this point. At the end of the writing time, members read their statement aloud, then all are collected and given to the writer.
I. The meeting concludes with discussion to determine:

• Whether the group believes it already has developed an effective statement to put forward.
• Whether the writer should return a single modified draft or two options

- What the writer should most keep in mind when developing the next draft(s).
- Who outside the group might be asked for feedback on the emerging statement or next draft(s).
- Setting the group's next meeting.

Step 5: Develop second drafts

Following the meeting, the writer or small subgroup develops a second draft of one or more possible new mission statements.

Step 6: Gain feedback from outside the writing group

This step puts the emerging statement or draft(s) to the test for their resonance with other members of the organization. The board chairman and chief executive decide who outside the writing group will be asked to give feedback. In some settings, organizationwide input is invited. In others, a smaller group of board members and staff is selected. There may also be value in gaining feedback from a few key informants outside the organization. The chief executive oversees the process of gaining feedback. If the board chairman is not already a member of the writing group, his or her feedback at this point is essential. Each individual or group being contacted for their response is:

A. Shown the criteria for an effective mission statement.
B. Asked for a rating of each draft, based on the criteria (meets, meets somewhat, doesn't meet).
C. Asked for comments on the merits and weaknesses of the draft(s).
D. Asked for ideas or recommendations for improvement.

Step 7: Summarize feedback and distribute second drafts and summary to writing group

Step 8: Propose a draft mission statement or determine next steps

With some groups, the process for developing a mission statement flows with ease to a unanimous and enthusiastic conclusion. With most, the process proves demanding but worthwhile when a strong statement emerges. A small number of groups come to feel they have been given the riddle of the Sphinx.

Mission-writing groups may choose to propose more than one statement for the board chairman or full board to consider, may ask for a board discussion to gain input and direction, or may simply go into another round of drafts and keep at it until the issue is resolved. If a group truly gets stuck, it may be helpful to let the task lie for a time and come back to it or take the challenge to a specialist outside the organization and gain a completely fresh perspective. As Peter Drucker reminds us, "What counts is not the beauty of the mission statement. What counts is your performance." It may, in the end, be most preferable to suggest an interim statement and live with it for a time before making a final decision.

At a third meeting, the writing group:

A. Reviews the emerging statement or second draft(s).
B. Hears and discusses a summary of feedback from outside the writing group.
C. Again rates the draft(s) against criteria and cites merits and weaknesses.
D. Attempts group editing or rewriting if there is agreement that they are "close and it's worth a try."
E. Determines if they have a strong enough draft to propose for approval.
    If so, the group makes final suggestions for fine-tuning and approves its proposed mission statement.
    If not, the group sums up the status of the process and recommends next steps.

Step 9: Gain preliminary endorsement of the proposed mission statement

If the mission is being revisited as part of a comprehensive organizational self-assessment process, preliminary endorsement by the board chairman is necessary before the Assessment Team confirms goals for the plan. The board chairman's preliminary endorsement is always necessary before he or she presents a proposed mission statement to the full board for approval.

Step 10: Present the proposed mission statement for board approval

The board chairman presents the proposed mission statement as part of the organization's plan or as a separate item of business. Approval of the mission is one of the board's most important responsibilities. If the board rejects a proposed mission, consideration of goals may have to be postponed until a mission is approved.

Sample Plans

Sample A   Vision, mission, goals to be presented by the board chairman for board approval; supporting budget to be presented by the chief executive for board approval

Sample B   Objectives to be presented to the board by the chief executive for information

Sample C   Vision, mission, goal, objectives, action steps for use by management

Sample A: Vision, mission, goals to be presented by the board chairman for board approval

STARS, Inc. Plan

Vision A prosperous region in which all residents have opportunities and support to develop their talents and sustain worthy employment.

Mission To fully develop the employment potential of the Southwest Region's people, employers, and communities.

Goals

1 Develop an extensive range of employment preparation and development services that produce long-term results and actively market them throughout the region.

2 Develop and market human-resource-related services to employers as, at minimum, a break-even venture.

3 Develop a diverse funding base and build a reserve fund.

4 Take a leadership role in shaping regional employment and training systems.

5 Strengthen the organization.

Sample A: Supporting budget to be presented by the chief executive for board approval

Goal 1

Operate and deliver JTPA-funded adult programs:	$1,775,517
Operate and deliver state youth programs:	$476,427
Operate and deliver dislocated worker programs:	$2,593,000
Develop new services and results tracking system:	$21,800

Goal 2

Develop business plan:	$7,260

Goal 3

New half-time development position:	$28,000

Goal 4

Operate and deliver welfare-to-work services:	$560,720
Develop and maintain cross-sector partnerships:	$15,000*
Pilot school-to-work program:	$20,000
Platform development and public relations:	$5,000*

Goal 5

Develop marketing plan:	$5,000
Enhance staff development activity:	$2,500
Subtotal existing programs:	$5,405,664
Subtotal new expenditures called for in plan:	$104,560
Total budget:	$5,510,224

*$20,000 already committed from Regional Grantmakers Futures Fund for innovations in regional welfare-to-work systems.

Sample B: Objectives to be presented to the board by the chief executive for information

STARS, Inc. Plan

Vision	A prosperous region in which all residents have opportunities and support to develop their talents and sustain worthy employment.
Mission	To fully develop the employment potential of the Southwest Region's people, employers, and communities.
Goal 1	Develop an extensive range of employment preparation and development services that produce long-term results and actively market them throughout the region.

Objective A: Continue to obtain available government contracts at federal, state, and county levels and exceed performance standards on annual basis.

Objective B: Develop measures to evaluate results in changed lives over extended time periods; implement tracking system in next fiscal year.

Objective C: Develop service enhancement plan and implement in next fiscal year.

Objective D: Show measurable improvement in customer service.

Goal 2   Develop and market human-resource-related services to employers as, at minimum, a break-even venture.

Objective A: Develop business plan.

Objective B: Obtain start-up funding and implement in next fiscal year.

Goal 3   Develop a diverse funding base and build a reserve fund.

Objective A: Develop internal financial management structures appropriate to a diverse financial base.

Objective B: Obtain private funding necessary to reach plan objectives.

Objective C: Set and achieve reserve fund targets for next three years.

Goal 4   Take a leadership role in shaping regional employment and training systems.

Objective A: Articulate a welfare-to-work and school-to-work platform.

Objective B: Develop and maintain cross-sector partnerships in each county.

Objective C: Demonstrate a successful track record in new welfare-to-work and school-to-work initiatives.

Objective D: Develop and implement a public relations plan that supports the STARS platform and conveys a leadership position.

Objective E: Expand effective services for welfare recipients and youth.

Goal 5   Strengthen the organization.

Objective A: Enhance board composition and performance.

Objective B: Develop and implement a staff development plan.

Objective C: Develop integrated annual marketing plans that achieve targets for recognition and response.

Sample C: Vision, mission, goal, objectives, action steps for use by management

STARS, Inc. Plan

Vision	A prosperous region in which all residents have opportunities and support to develop their talents and sustain worthy employment.
Mission	To fully develop the employment potential of the Southwest Region's people, employers, and communities.
Goal 1	Develop an extensive range of employment preparation and development services that produce long-term results and actively market them throughout the region.

Objective A: Continue to obtain available government contracts at federal, state, and county levels and exceed performance standards on annual basis.

Step	Who's Responsible	Appraisal
1. Submit proposals for renewal of annual contracts.	Per assignment; planner coordinates	Annual; March deadlines
2. Monitor new federal, state, and county initiatives and submit proposals as opportunities arise.	Executive director	Quarterly
3. Maintain existing performance evaluation system and extend to new contracts.	Deputy director	Monthly

Objective B: Develop ability to evaluate results over extended time periods; implement tracking system in next fiscal year.

Step	Who's Responsible	Appraisal
1. Survey "best practices" in employment and training organizations nationally.	Deputy director	Oct 1
2. Develop draft recommendations for what results should be and system for measurement.	Deputy director	Feb 1
3. Present report to management team for discussion.	Deputy director	Feb 15

Step	Who's Responsible	Appraisal
4. Amend/endorse recommendations.	Management team	Apr 1
5. Present recommendations for what results should be for discussion.	Executive director to board	May 1
6. Implement system.	Executive director	Jul 1
7. Report results to board.	Executive director	Annually

Objective C: Develop service enhancement plan and implement in next fiscal year.

Step	Who's Responsible	Appraisal
1. Conduct and analyze market research to determine target audiences, types and levels of interest and need, pricing, competition, and potential partners and funders.	Planner, consultant	Jan 1
2. Determine service and staff development needs in light of market research and best practices research (see Objective B, Step 2).	Job training manager	Feb 1
3. Develop service enhancement plan.	Planner, job training manager, executive director, new marketing and development staff	
4. Present plan for board dis-. cussion	Executive director	May 1
5. Implement plan.	Executive director	July 1
6. Report to board on plan performance.	Executive director	Semi-annually

Objective D: Show measurable improvement in customer service.

Step	Who's Responsible	Appraisal
1. Resolve difficulty with job placement service or implement alternative	Executive director	Dec 1

Step	Who's Responsible	Appraisal
2. Form and lead Service Excellence Task Force to develop measures, establish baseline, develop implementation plans for immediate improvements, and recommend system for on-going appraisal.	Planner	Dec 1
3. Present report to executive director.	Planner and task force	Mar 1
4. Amend/approve recommendations and implement.	Executive director	Apr 1

Recommended Reading

Building Community

Drucker, P. F. *Post-Capitalist Society.* New York: HarperCollins, 1994.

Hesselbein, F., Goldsmith, M., Beckhard, R., and Schubert, R. (eds.). *The Community of the Future.* San Francisco: Jossey-Bass, 1998.

Kahn, S. *How People Get Power.* National Association of Social Workers, 1994.

Kretzman J., and McKnight, J. L. *Building Communities from the Inside Out: A Path Toward Finding and Mobilizing a Community's Assets.* Chicago: ACTA, 1997.

Mattessich, P., and Monsey, B. R. *Collaboration: What Makes It Work.* St. Paul, Minn.: Amherst H. Wilder Foundation, 1992.

Mattessich, P., and Monsey, B. R. *Community Building: What Makes It Work: A Review of Factors Influencing Successful Community Building.* St. Paul, Minn.: Amherst H. Wilder Foundation, 1997.

McCarthy, K. D. *The Nonprofit Sector in the Global Community: Voices from Many Nations.* San Francisco: Jossey-Bass, 1992.

Schorr, L. *Common Purpose: Strengthening Families and Neighborhoods to Rebuild America.* New York: Doubleday, 1997.

Toqueville, A. *Democracy in America.* Vols. 1 and 2. New York: Vintage Books, 1990.

Leading the Organization

Carver, J. *Boards That Make a Difference: A New Design for Leadership in Nonprofit and Public Organizations.* San Francisco: Jossey-Bass, 1997.

Helgesen, S. *The Web of Inclusion.* New York: Doubleday, 1995.

Hesselbein, F., Goldsmith, M., and Beckhard, R. (eds.). *The Leader of the Future.* San Francisco: Jossey-Bass, 1996.

Hesselbein, F., Goldsmith, M., and Beckhard, R. (eds.). *The Organization of the Future.* San Francisco: Jossey-Bass, 1997.

James, J. *Thinking in the Future Tense: Leadership Skills for a New Age.* New York: Simon & Schuster, 1996.

Wheatley, M. J. *Leadership and the New Science: Learning About Organization from an Orderly Universe.* San Francisco: Berrett-Koehler, 1992.

Managing the Organization

Drucker, P. F. *Managing the Non-Profit Organization: Practices and Principles.* New York: HarperCollins, 1992.

Drucker, P. F. *Management: Tasks, Responsibilities, Practices.* New York: Harper-Collins, 1993.

Drucker, P. F. *Managing in a Time of Great Change.* New York: Truman Talley Books, 1995.

Haltry, H., van Houten, T., Plantz, M. C., and Taylor, M. *Measuring Program Outcomes: A Practical Approach.* Alexandria, Va.: United Way of America, 1996. (To order: Sales Service/America, 1-800-772-0008.)

Katzenbach, J. R., and Smith, D. K. *The Wisdom of Teams: Creating the High-Performance Organization.* New York: HarperCollins, 1993.

Kotler, P., and Andreasen, A. R. *Strategic Marketing for Nonprofit Organizations.* Englewood Cliffs, N.J.: Prentice Hall, 1995.

Patton, M. Q. *Utilization-Focused Evaluation: The New Century Text.* Thousand Oaks, Calif.: Sage, 1996.

Prince, R. A., and File, K. M. *The Seven Faces of Philanthropy: A New Approach to Cultivating Major Donors.* San Francisco: Jossey-Bass, 1994.

Senge, P. M. *The Fifth Discipline Fieldbook: Strategies and Tools for Building a Learning Organization.* New York: Doubleday, 1994.

Smith, D. K. *Taking Charge of Change: 10 Principles for Managing People and Performance.* Reading, Mass.: Addison-Wesley, 1996.

Stern, G. J. *Marketing Workbook for Nonprofit Organizations,* Vol. I: *Develop the Marketing Plan.* St. Paul, Minn.: Amherst H. Wilder Foundation, 1990.

Stern, G. J. *Marketing Workbook for Nonprofit Organizations,* Vol. II: *Mobilize People for Marketing Success.* St. Paul, Minn.: Amherst H. Wilder Foundation, 1997.

Steering the Self-Assessment Process

Hagberg, J., and Donovan, T. *Learning Styles Inventory.* Plymouth, Minn.: Personal Power Products, 1996.

Hunter, D., Bailey, A., and Taylor, B. *Zen of Groups: A Handbook for People Meeting with a Purpose.* Tucson, Ariz.: Fisher Books, 1995.

Lukas, C. *Consulting with Nonprofits: A Practitioner's Guide.* St. Paul, Minn.: Amherst H. Wilder Foundation, 1990.

About the
Drucker Foundation

The Peter F. Drucker Foundation for Nonprofit Management, founded in 1990, takes its name and inspiration from the acknowledged father of modern management. By providing educational opportunities and resources, the foundation furthers its mission "to lead social sector organizations toward excellence in performance." It pursues this mission through the presentation of conferences, video teleconferences, the annual Peter F. Drucker Award for Nonprofit Innovation, and the annual Frances Hesselbein Community Innovation Fellows Program, as well as through the development of management resources, partnerships, and publications.

Since its founding, the Drucker Foundation's special role has been to serve as a broker of intellectual capital, bringing together the finest leaders, consultants, authors, and social philosophers in the world with the leaders of social sector voluntary organizations.

The Drucker Foundation believes that a healthy society requires three vital sectors: a public sector of effective governments, a private sector of effective businesses, and a social sector of effective community organizations. The mission of the social sector and its organizations is to change lives. It accomplishes this mission by addressing the needs of the spirit, mind, and body of individuals, the community, and society. This sector and its organizations also create a meaningful sphere of effective and responsible citizenship.

The Drucker Foundation aims to make its contribution to the health of society by strengthening the social sector through the provision of intellectual resources to leaders in business, government, and the social sector. In the first seven years after its inception, the Drucker Foundation, among other things:

- Presented the Drucker Innovation Award, which each year generates several hundred applications from local community enterprises; many applicants work in fields where results are difficult to achieve.

- Held twenty conferences in the United States and in countries across the world.

- Developed four books; three books in the Drucker Foundation Future Series are *The Leader of the Future* (1996), *The Organization of the Future* (1997), and *The Community of the Future* (1998).

- Developed *Leader to Leader*, a quarterly journal for leaders from all three sectors.
- Assisted in the development of similar organizations in Argentina and Canada.

If you would like more information on the Drucker Foundation and its programs and publications, please write, call, FAX, or e-mail the foundation at:

The Peter F. Drucker Foundation for Nonprofit Management
320 Park Avenue, 3rd Floor
New York, NY 10022-6839
Telephone: (212) 224-1174
Fax: (212) 224-2508
E-mail: info@pfdf.org
Web address: www.pfdf.org

The foundation's Web site includes dates and locations of self-assessment training workshops, and additional resources to inform and guide Assessment Teams and participants.

Self-Assessment Tool
Customer Feedback Form

This revised edition of *The Drucker Foundation Self-Assessment Tool* was produced with significant input from our customers. Your feedback as a customer is very important in appraising the success of the *Tool,* in determining how it can best be introduced to others, and in considering new resources the Drucker Foundation might offer. We hope you will take a few minutes to complete the survey and return it to us by mail or fax. You can also complete this survey on our Web site at www.pfdf.org.

I. Tell us about your organization.

1. Year founded: _____

2. Annual operating budget:
   - ☐ Less than $100,000
   - ☐ $100,001 to $500,000
   - ☐ $500,001 to $2,000,000
   - ☐ $2,000,001 to $10,000,000
   - ☐ More than $10,000,000

3. Is your organization a
   - ☐ Nonprofit
   - ☐ Unit of government
   - ☐ For-profit business

4. In which area or areas does your organization work? (Check as many as apply.)
   - ☐ Arts, culture
   - ☐ Community development
   - ☐ Education
   - ☐ Employment/job opportunities
   - ☐ Environment
   - ☐ Health
   - ☐ Human service
   - ☐ Management training/consulting
   - ☐ Philanthropic/foundation
   - ☐ Religious/spiritual
   - ☐ Youth service
   - ☐ Other _____

5. Which best describes your organization's service area?
   - ☐ Urban center
   - ☐ Suburban area
   - ☐ Small town
   - ☐ Metropolitan area
   - ☐ Region
   - ☐ State
   - ☐ Nation
   - ☐ International
   - ☐ Other _____

6. Does your organization primarily serve an ethnic, racial, or culturally specific constituency?

☐ Yes   ☐ No

If yes, please identify constituency:

II. Tell us about your experience with the *Self-Assessment Tool.*

7. How did you first hear about *The Drucker Foundation Self-Assessment Tool?*

☐ In mailings from the publisher (Jossey-Bass)
☐ At a self-assessment training workshop
☐ At a conference
☐ By word of mouth
☐ Read an article or review about it
☐ Saw an advertisement for it
☐ At Drucker Foundation Web site
☐ Other _____

8. How have you used the *Self-Assessment Tool?* (Check as many as apply.)

☐ Read the materials
☐ Used one or more exercises
☐ Applied the ideas or concepts in my work
☐ Conducted a self-assessment process
☐ Other _____

If your organization did not conduct a self-assessment process, please skip to question 11.

9. In your organization's self-assessment process, did you use a facilitator?

☐ No
☐ Yes, we used an outside facilitator
☐ Yes, we used a facilitator from inside the organization
☐ Yes, we used both outside and inside facilitators

10. Do you agree or disagree with the following statements:

The *Self-Assessment Tool* helped us:	Agree	Agree somewhat	Disagree
a. Structure and complete an organizational planning process.	☐	☐	☐
b. Identify our customers.	☐	☐	☐
c. Determine what our customers value.	☐	☐	☐
d. Clarify our organizational goals.	☐	☐	☐
e. Define what our results should be.	☐	☐	☐
f. Determine how we will measure results.	☐	☐	☐
g. Deepen understanding of our mission.	☐	☐	☐
h. Develop common vision and unity of direction.	☐	☐	☐

11. Are there any other comments you would like to make about the *Self-Assessment Tool,* about its Process Guide or Participant Workbook, or about your organization's experience with it?

III. Tell us about you.

Name _____

Organization _____

Address _____

City _____ State _____ Zip _____

Telephone _____ Fax _____ E-mail _____

12. Would you be willing to be listed in a Drucker Foundation database of organizations that have used the *Self-Assessment Tool,* and to share your experience with others?
    ☐ Yes   ☐ No

13. Would your organization be interested in sponsoring a Drucker Foundation Self-Assessment Training Workshop in your area?
    ☐ Yes   ☐ No

14. Would you be willing to participate in future customer surveys on the *Tool*?

☐ Yes ☐ No

15. Would you like to be added to our mailing list for information on our publications, conferences, and resources?

☐ Yes ☐ No

16. Would you or another individual who facilitated self-assessment with your organization like to be listed in a Drucker Foundation database of facilitators? The Drucker Foundation does not certify or endorse self-assessment facilitators.

☐ Yes ☐ No

Name of facilitator _____

Organization _____

Address _____

City _____ State _____ Zip _____

Telephone _____ Fax _____ E-mail _____

For information, readings, and resources, see the Drucker Foundation Web site at www.pfdf.org. Please return this form to:

The Drucker Foundation
320 Park Avenue, 3rd Floor
New York, NY 10022-6839 USA

Telephone: (212) 224-1174

Fax: (212) 224-2508

E-mail: info@pfdf.org

Web address: www.pfdf.org